The Humanities and Public Life

The Humanities and Public Life

Edited by PETER BROOKS

with HILARY JEWETT

FORDHAM UNIVERSITY PRESS

New York 2014

Library of Congress Cataloging-in-Publication Data

The humanities and public life / edited by Peter Brooks
    with Hilary Jewett. — First edition.
        pages cm
    Includes bibliographical references.
    ISBN 978-0-8232-5704-1 (cloth : alk. paper) —
    ISBN 978-0-8232-5705-8 (pbk. : alk. paper)
    1. Humanities—Moral and ethical aspects. 2. Reading—
Moral and ethical aspects. 3. Human rights—Moral and
ethical aspects. I. Brooks, Peter, 1938– editor of
compilation. II. Jewett, Hilary, editor of compilation.
    AZ103.H846 2014
    001.3—dc23

                                          2013025465

Printed in the United States of America

16 15 14 5 4 3 2 1

First edition

CONTENTS

ACKNOWLEDGMENTS

Convening the symposium "The Humanities in the Public Sphere" and then making from it the present book demanded much effort from several people. Our thanks go first to the participants, who responded to the call to contribute short position papers and pointed responses with fresh and pertinent thinking. Thanks next go to the audience, which engaged speakers and respondents in debate that was usually sharp, helpful, and worth recording. The symposium owed much to the support of Kim Lane Scheppele, Director of the Program in Law and Public Affairs at Princeton, and to Leslie Gerwin, Judi Rivkin, and Jennifer Bolton. It was also supported by Charles Beitz, Director of the University Center for Human Values, with help from Erum Syed, Susan Winters, and Kimberly Girman, and backed by Leonard Barkan, Chair of Comparative Literature, and Cheryl Cantore, manager of that department. Many last-minute arrangements were graciously handled by Dora Zhang.

We are grateful also to Helen Tartar, editorial director of Fordham University Press, for her quick and enthusiastic endorsement of our book, and unflagging encouragement in seeing it through to publication. We are also grateful to assistant editor Thomas Lay.

Reaching further back, neither symposium nor book would have been possible without the very generous award from the Andrew W. Mellon Foundation that, in 2008, gave birth to the series of seminars known as "The Ethics of Reading and the Cultures of Professionalism," which from the start envisioned this symposium as their point of arrival (though they in fact continue to this day). Special thanks are due to Harriet Zuckerman and Joseph Meisel, the pillars of the humanities at the foundation.

While the conception of seminars, symposium, and book was the work of Peter Brooks, Hilary Jewett was coordinator throughout and performed the editorial work on this volume.

Introduction

Peter Brooks

Over the past few years, I have taught a seminar for students and faculty under the title "The Ethics of Reading and the Cultures of Professionalism." The seminar asked these questions: What leverage does reading of the attentive sort practiced in the humanities give one on life? Does such reading represent or produce an ethics? Should such an ethics of reading inhabit professional training and the public sphere as well? These questions were posed for me with brutal force after reading the "Torture Memos" released by the U.S. Department of Justice, in the years following their composition in 2002.[1] These documents presented arguments that justified the use of torture by the most twisted, ingenious, perverse, and unethical interpretation of legal texts. Many others have taken apart these memoranda from the Office of Legal Counsel—supposed to provide the highest standard of legal analysis—so I will not detail here how they interpret the meaning and usage of words and phrases in ways that are arbitrary and authoritarian rather than probative. No one trained in the rigorous analysis of poetry, I said to myself, could possibly engage in such bad-faith interpretation without professional conscience intervening to say: this is not right. That was the position that I tried to stake out in the seminar, all the while knowing that it could not be taken as an article of faith, that it needed exploration and analysis if not proof. That seminar (to which I brought a number of distinguished visitors) led to and called for the "The Humanities in the Public Sphere" symposium, which furnished the material for this book.

The issue of the Torture Memos and my classroom experience in interpreting legal texts led me to the claim that the humanities can, and at their best do, represent a commitment to ethical reading. This commitment, and the training and discipline of close reading that underlies it, represents something that we as teachers of the humanities need to bring to other fields, especially those that undertake the training of professional readers such as lawyers, whose work includes interpretation.

Teaching the humanities appears to many to be a disempowered profession with reduced status within American culture. The widespread perception of a crisis of the humanities is the most acute manifestation of a crisis of American higher education in general. So we have been told by countless books that have been rolling out since the 1980s, from *Profscam* and *Tenured Radicals* to *Academically Adrift* and *Higher Education?*[2] In 2011, the *New York Review of Books* entitled an article by my colleague Anthony Grafton "Our Flunking Universities."[3] The very value of a university education, for so many decades a central article of American faith, now has been put into doubt. The whole enterprise, we are told, may be a waste of time, money, and national commitment. There is even a philanthropic organization—the Thiel Foundation—that offers prizes of $100,000 to induce smart kids to drop out of college and become entrepreneurs on their own, on the theory that college impedes rather than enhances the development of creative ideas. In this "crisis," the humanities are made to appear a kind of zombie wandering in a world that should be producing technocrats and entrepreneurs.

But the crisis may truly lie elsewhere, in the marginalization of humanistic thought and analysis. The ability to read critically the messages that society, politics, and culture bombard us with is, more than ever, needed training in a society in which the manipulation of minds and hearts is increasingly what running the world is all about. We who practice the interpretive humanities need to be less modest, and to stake a claim to the public importance of our task. Shelley was not entirely wrong to insist that poets are the unacknowledged legislators of mankind: Cultural change carries everything in its wake. The close reading practiced in the humanities ought to be an export commodity to other fields, and it should take its place in public life.

My own field is literary study, and what I have said so far sounds as if I were interested only in literary analysis and interpretation. In fact, I would argue that the close, intense, disciplined reading crucial to literary study underlies the humanities as a whole: The "interpretive turn" of philosophy in our time has had its cognates across the range of humanistic disciplines. Very often, humanistic interpretation starts from a specific act of reading—of a document difficult to decipher, a word needing to be glossed, a fragment of an artifact needing reconstruction, a visual detail suggestive of iconographic meaning, an idea begging for context—and moves from there to larger interpretive structures and theories. Insofar as the humanities are an interpretive enterprise—as they mostly are, when not engaged in simpler forms of data gathering—they cannot do without reading of a careful, analytic, self-conscious kind.

I began by evoking the Torture Memos because in that case the disastrous results of not reading—of merely pretending to read while in fact inserting one's own prejudices and preferred outcomes between the reader and the text—are so clear and so horrible. To misread the Convention Against Torture and Cruel and Inhuman Treatment, as incorporated in the U.S. Legal Code, shows in a consequential way what bad-faith interpretation can produce. Though the consequences of other sloppy, misguided, pernicious interpretations may not be so spectacularly awful, they can skew everything that follows in their wake. The *New Yorker* journalist Jane Mayer claimed that the Bush administration began its distortion of reality with the distortion of language.[4] That seems to me profoundly true, not only in that specific case but in contemporary culture in general.

This should not be construed as a call for single meanings of complex texts, a flight from ambiguity and uncertainty. On the contrary, reading as a self-conscious practice—"reading in slow motion," as it has been called—tends to suggest the inadequacies of the simple and the certain. I do not believe, either, that reading good books necessarily makes one a good person. There are plenty of examples from our history to give the lie to that idea: People can spend the day killing Jews and go home to read Goethe in the evening. What I want to defend is not a product but a process and a practice. The practice of reading itself, pursued with care and attention to language, its contexts, implications, uncertainties, can itself be an ethical act. To make sure that our interpretation can be defended in the context of the text (and its contexts) means that—unlike the authors of the Torture Memos—we must constantly submit what we want the text to mean to the constraints of the lexicon, the historical horizon, and the text as a whole. This submission to culture as something beyond one's individuality is in itself a discipline. It is a version of what T. S. Eliot meant when he claimed that all great art is impersonal.

I have not quite finished with the question of reading as a practice, in the classroom and elsewhere; I will say more about it later. But I want to come to the other voices in this volume. My thoughts about the ethics of reading led me to the idea of a symposium on the subject and to the gathering of this exceptional group of people. My premises and speculations needed testing by a range of thinkers whose work crosses from the practice of reading to large ethical and social concerns. I sent those I invited to participate instructions stating my goals for the meeting, exhorting them to write focused, pointed comments on the topics raised. This was not to be a meeting where professors came to read scholarly papers, but an exchange of views, a conversation. Each talk was to be no more than fifteen minutes, and for each of the three sessions there would be two speakers and two or three respondents, then general discussion with the audience. So the oral exchange (largely included here) was really just as important as the written statements.

To start the symposium, I thought we should have a keynote talk of somewhat greater length by someone whose work was recognized by all as crossing in crucial ways from the practices of reading into public life. Hence, Judith Butler presented (to a predictably overflow crowd) her lecture "Ordinary, Incredulous," which responds to the occasion by addressing a critical issue in our understanding of and wish to defend the humanities: How do we defend our practices without using the very language and the very framework of values of those who wish to see knowledge in purely instrumental terms? The conception of knowledge as essentially instrumental, as measured by its worldly use value, dominates talk about education worldwide at present. Even if to us—the kind of people who talked and listened at the symposium—the value of the humanities is obvious and in need of defense, we imperil our commitments if we reply to our detractors that we will not bother to answer their critiques, if we take any defense of the use of the humanities off the table. Yet when we do undertake that defense, we can quickly be caught up in the very language of instrumentality that has contested our worth. One cannot argue the intrinsic worth of the humanities to those who simply cannot recognize it. But, asks Butler, "If the humanities are to make a difference in public life, does that mean we have to say that they are instrumental to some other social good? Is instrumentality the only way we have of thinking about what it means to make a difference?"

Here we are at a crux that anyone in the academy recognizes as real and present. Faculty in the United Kingdom, subject for some years now to the "Research Assessment Exercise," have been forced to demonstrate the "impact" of their work, the social outcomes that can be expected from it. In the United States, a movement well-funded by various foundations and think tanks urges that universities test the "outcomes" of the education they provide and charge tuition for, that they measure the "value added" by a college education. A profitable testing industry has developed, touting such metrics as the College Learning Assessment, which aims to offer grounds for comparison of the effectiveness of various programs and institutions. I will come back to these tests, which appear to define knowledge "outcomes" as largely instrumental, as problem solving. They do not begin to test the kinds of understanding taught in the humanities. To use a grandiose and unfashionable but perhaps apt word, they do not test wisdom.

As Butler writes further, "our very capacity for critically re-evaluating is what cannot be measured by the metrics by which the humanities are increasingly judged." The query she received in response to a grant proposal—"what is the deliverable of your proposal?"—leads Butler into a dazzling riff on the notion of "the deliverable," as precisely the instrumentalization of knowledge into a package that can arrive on someone's doorstep. By the end of her discussion, she has reposed the question in stark terms: "We find ourselves housed and displaced within language with metrics of value that not only cannot gauge well what we do, but have so monopolized the field of value that they threaten to consign what we do to oblivion." Resistance to oblivion means re-posing the question of values, questioning the obvious, and refusing instrumental metrics while keeping in play a critical relation to the kinds of contemporary deployments of language that Butler holds up to examination.

I respond to Butler's analysis with something like awe at her dialectical abilities and her capacity to draw an audience into a mode of thinking that precisely demonstrates the kind of resistance that must be exercised. She offers a sinuous and persuasive argument that must be followed through the detail of its movement: It is not designed to produce a packaged "deliverable" but rather a form of critical thinking. As an initiation into the kind of attention our topic needs, Butler's essay is exemplary.

The symposium continued with three sessions followed by a final round-table. The first session addressed the underlying assumption on which I had been working—though also questioning—in my seminar: "Is There an Ethics of Reading?" What do we learn when we read in self-conscious awareness of the interpretive process? The interpreter, etymologically and still today, is a go-between, a kind of ambassador of meanings who brings an effort at understanding from one region to another. Why, we may well want to ask, is interpretation necessary? Why does understanding of the written necessarily activate the go-between role of the interpreter? Why can't meanings simply be read off? What does the need to interpret teach us about language itself, about its role in regulating and defining the human? Elaine Scarry, a literary scholar of wide reach, and Charles Larmore, a philosopher, address these issues in very different ways, yet both, I think, are directly on target. Scarry directs our attention to the long tradition of poetry that is deliberative and argumentative, that stages a dispute or dialogue of two voices. By way of this formal structure of poetry, she extends claims about reading's capacity to inculcate empathy—as in Lynn Hunt's contention that human rights discourse really derives from the eighteenth-century novel.[5] This in turn moves to Scarry's concern with beauty as creating a responsive capacity within us. Her essay begins with the question of whether reading diminishes the injuries of the world, but by the time she has worked through her argument the answer must clearly be yes—not in any simple sense (not that reading makes us better people), but rather in the capacity of reading (perhaps only reading) to nourish that which makes us human.

Charles Larmore directs us to a problem identified by Plato in his *Phaedrus:* that texts "roam about everywhere" and are subject to readings and misreadings by anyone, without the author at hand to offer correction. This perception leads Larmore to a meditation on the ways in which reading might be said to implicate ethical relations. If a text cannot be protected from misreadings—and if in any case we would not necessarily accept the author's own reading of the text as definitive—what does this say about the careful relation that a reader ought to establish with a text? In closing, Larmore cites Karl Kraus on the respect for language, as a "mental discipline that enjoins the highest measure of responsibility toward the sole thing that can be wronged with impunity, namely language, and that serves like no other to teach respect for every other kind of human good." That sense of "responsibility" toward language, which of course includes respect for how it works in any given utterance addressed to us, very directly goes to the issues of an ethics of reading that most concern me.

Larmore's insistence that the ethical relation of reading need stand in relation to an author, a person, and not simply to a text brings a measure of dissent from the respondents Kwame Anthony Appiah, philosopher, and Derek Attridge, literary scholar, who offer reinterpretations of who or what it is that we may feel responsible to in the act of reading. Jonathan Culler, a literary theorist, on the other hand, dismisses the notion of an ethics of reading as an attempt by literary critics to rescue their work from the charge of nihilism or futility. Texts "roaming about everywhere" may be subject to all sorts of uses. I find my own sympathies falling in line with Attridge's careful modifications of Larmore's thesis, which lead him to a restatement that emphasizes that writing a text is an act in which one makes oneself "vulnerable" to others—and that our treatment of the vulnerable is a test of our ethical character. This, for Attridge, touches on the ethical thinking of Emmanuel Levinas, based on our recognition of and responsibility for the other. If texts represent an attempt—fragile, vulnerable—by someone else to communicate with us, we might conceive our responsibility to be one of respectful attention to the communication. To me, this does not necessarily entail evocation of the person or persons who created the text—who are largely inaccessible as persons—but to the act of attempted communication itself.

My original title for the seminar, "The Ethics of Reading and the Cultures of Professionalism," indicated my concern that the kinds of reading practiced in the humanities at their best might need to be more strongly represented in professional education if we are seeking to prevent the types of readings found in the Torture Memos. So in our second session we turned to "The Ethics of Reading and the Professions." Professional education may be the most characteristic and powerful product of the modern American university. Has the drive to professionalization—as found, for instance, in the emergence of modern American law and business schools—suppressed attention to an ethics of reading? Do humanistic traditions of reading need to be better represented in professional schools? Would a more rhetorically aware pedagogy of reading provide a useful corrective to largely pragmatic assumptions about language? Once upon a time, the high-ranking British civil servant tended to have been recruited from the study of classical "greats" at Oxford or Cambridge. This model never quite obtained in the United States, and it seems quaint today. But it may be important to ask whether there are ways to create a new and forceful public relevance of the kind of reading, interpretation, and reflection that constitute the humanities at their best.

Our speakers on this subject were Patricia Williams of Columbia Law School—who is also a columnist for *The Nation* as well as someone who has intervened decisively in American political discourse, especially on issues of race—and Ralph Hexter, trained as a classicist, who is currently the provost and vice chancellor at the University of California–Davis. In her paper, Williams summons every reader to consider his or her captioning of the world, and she herself performs a cultural reading of responses, including captions and fictions, to extreme events. Hexter then situates reading within a corporate and collective context where interpretive outcomes and their ethical effects matter very much in people's lives. In this context, he forcefully proposes that "as readers—that is, as interpreters— we should skew deontological. . . . That is to say, we should be ethical in our process rather than use ends to justify unethical means." In response, Michael Roth, the President of Wesleyan University, offers a provocation: The turn to an ethics of reading may in his view mark an avoidance maneuver, a flight from playful and violent reading, which he associates with the heyday of deconstruction. The ethical does not, in my view, exclude playfulness—one could reach back to Schiller's *Letters on the Aesthetic Education of Mankind* to argue that play lies at the heart of any aesthetic reading—but I must register a deep disagreement on violence, which does not seem to me a serious option. We came back to these questions at the end of the day.

Richard Sennett, a sociologist, urbanist, and cultural critic, in turn evokes the potentially tragic circumstance in which art, playfulness, self-expression, and reading (in my sense) might only find support and a place for their exercise in a few elite institutions. William Germano, sometime editor at Routledge and Columbia and currently the Dean of Humanities at Cooper Union, directs us to the relation of writers and readers as essentially ethical: "Write as if you mean it, and write as if what you write can change the reader. Because it will." A summons to which I think most of the participants would assent.

In our third session, we took on the problematic and currently much-debated relation of the humanities to human rights. Humanists do not necessarily teach the humanitarian. I think it only promotes confusion to claim that studying the humanities makes one more humane—there are plenty of examples from throughout history to the contrary. Though we surely want to promote the reading of good books, we should beware of assuming they have beneficial results. And great books, from *Job* and *Oedipus the King* to *Moby-Dick* and *The Brothers Karamazov* have in fact always given a large place to dissent from conventional virtue and the pretty picture of human life. The humanities as we know them largely descend from Renaissance humanism's concern to restore ancient texts and to learn to read them. The enterprise of the *literae humaniores* is human in that it deals with human reflections on the human condition. It is not necessarily on the side of what we would consider right thinking about human rights.

To what extent can humanistic learning provide the basis for reflection on human rights? Is the form of imaginative sympathy promoted by literature and its attentive reading indeed foundational for human rights discourse? I mentioned earlier the argument advanced by historian Lynn Hunt in her book *Inventing Human Rights* that the concept of human rights really derives from eighteenth-century literature, primarily from the novel—and most of all the epistolary novels of Samuel Richardson and Jean-Jacques Rousseau—that teach us to put ourselves imaginatively in the place of others. That, too, was the argument of Adam Smith in his *Theory of Moral Sentiments*. What the eighteenth century called "sympathy" or "pity," and we tend to call "empathy," derives from this capacity to see and feel the world from another's point of view. Our noticing of violations of human dignity has been decisively promoted by fiction, from Harriet Beecher Stowe's *Uncle Tom's Cabin* to J. M. Coetzee's *Waiting for the Barbarians*. Yet may there not be limits to an understanding of rights based on fictional identifications? Rousseau himself warns us of the dangers inherent in the capacity to simulate emotions: The simulation itself can satisfy, and unsettle our moral compass.

Speaking to these questions were Jonathan Lear, philosopher and psychoanalyst, and Paul Kahn, a legal scholar whose work has ranged from analyses of *Marbury v. Madison* to *King Lear*. Jonathan Lear gives an arresting account of how the words of the last great chief of the Crow Indians provoked a reaction in him—some fifteen years after hearing them—that led to his engagement with the Crow in a joint philosophical and psychoanalytic interpretive effort to come to terms with a grievous loss of cultural identity. Lear's account here represents an exemplary connection of interpretive skill and ethical commitment—putting one's life into the consequences of one's interpretive acts. Lear draws clearly the pertinence of his argument to our topic: The measuring tools of the social scientists (the Crow have been much studied by them) are inadequate to a full understanding of cultural devastation and the loss of a belief system. Only the interpretive reading of the humanities can begin to foster this understanding. When Lear calls for a "poetic" response to the harms inflicted on Crow culture by the dominant American culture, he understands poetry to mean words that can awake us from complacency and lethargy, to make us see the world anew.

Paul Kahn offers a skeptical view of human rights law as a universal consensus grounded in sympathy for the pain of others and agreement to prevent it. The political imagination values not only sympathy but sacrifice, and that promotes violence. To Kahn, the humanities can provide something that the law and social science cannot: the act of interpretation as itself an act of creation. He makes the important point that "the truth of an interpretation is not separate from the act of interpretation." That is, the making of an interpretation—which can only be answered by another interpretation, in a potentially endless conversation—needs to be judged not only on its product but on how it is carried out. A belief in human dignity, according to Kahn, needs to be based not in sympathy for the suffering of others but in the shared mystery of human creativity.

Responses came from Kim Lane Scheppele, the director of Princeton's Law and Public Affairs Program, and Didier Fassin, professor in the School of Social Science at the Institute for Advanced Study, whose work has led him from Doctors Without Borders to anthropology and the politics of humanitarian intervention. Scheppele, starting from Kahn's defense of human creativity, considers the meaning of self-authorship as a claim to the dignity of individuals. Here, she calls on her knowledge of Russia and Eastern Europe, and the practices of resistance to totalitarianism through irony, quotation, and musical dissonance—tactics or techniques that Sergei Oushakine calls "mimetic resistance." Within a space that the state wishes to close and police, creativity is an interpretation and an act of defiance. Didier Fassin, from his engagement with humanitarian intervention efforts and with the issues of human rights, offers both a defense and a critique of the humanities, and a proposal for creative dialogue between social sciences and humanistic thinking. If the "imaginary of human rights and humanitarianism is saturated with the generous ambition of the good one can do for others by defending and assisting them," this needs to be subject to critical thinking, for it can produce harm as well as good. The human rights claim can trump and obscure political claims to basic rights. That Fassin ends by citing Kurtz in Conrad's *Heart of Darkness*, the emissary of a colonialist "progress," beautifully turns the problem, for Kurtz is precisely the humanitarian imagination gone mad.

We reserved time for discussion with all the panelists—and the audience—at the end of each session and for a roundtable at the end of the day. In these discussions, we came back often to what was always the central question of the symposium: Can we claim that there is an ethics in the humanities, derivable from the kind of work done in the humanities? Jonathan Culler and Michael Roth had delivered especially negative judgments on this issue, and I agree with them that the ethics that may be derivable from the humanities is no simple matter. Learning "the best that has been thought and said in the world," to quote Matthew Arnold's defense of culture, does not create an ethics, though it might be a necessary precondition for intelligent ethical thinking. But as I have already suggested, I think the issue needs to be reframed, not as one concerning the outcome of reading but rather the very practice of reading. As Paul Kahn observed in his remarks, the truth of interpretation in the humanities cannot be separated from the *act* of interpretation.

It is my own view that the teacher of literature (and this can be true as well for the teacher of philosophy or art history or music, for instance) has the strange experience of not speaking quite with or in his or her own voice. In the classroom, we let other voices, from the past for instance, speak through us. As interpreters, we are mouthpieces of others—we are ventriloquists of the ideas and words of others. This experience of otherness—perhaps an experience akin to what Keats called "negative capability," the capacity of the poet to inhabit other personalities and perspectives—seems to me characteristic of reading and interpretation in the humanities, and it leads to a certain ethics: a self-dispossession in favor of the text, another voice in the room. That text, of course, can also be a painting or a potsherd or a musical phrase, and the object of interpretation shares the stage with the interpreter. At its best, such an attitude allows the voice of the other to develop its full force, its full articulation, without censoring it—in a kind of dualism of feeling. When class begins, the text or the artifact may appear absent or mute; it is our job to try to give it voice: not our voice but one we create from our understanding of it so that students can enter into dialogue with it. We, as teachers, are speaking in dialogue with another voice, which we try to make present in the classroom with full justice to its claims in order that we may make the dialogue just.

The discipline of close reading thus lies in this attempted fidelity to another voice or presence, perhaps more accurately the animation of this voice or presence through our own speech acts. I come close here to Larmore's claim that the reader must engage an "author," but I think it is not so much a real as a projected or imputed author, something like one of Henry James's ghosts. To insist that the reader encounter an author is to discount too much the mediating practices of textuality, of convention and genre. We re-create, to the best of our investigative, analytic, and imaginative ability, that putative author to whom we impute intentions of meaning. Reading in this sense is very much the discipline of a *practice*— not a nugget of content or a lesson taken from what is read, but what we discover *in the reading process itself,* in the disciplined effort to come to terms with what that text means.

When we talk of "sympathy" and "empathy" as central to the experience of studying the textual humanities—very often the basis of the claim that the understanding of human rights originates in the understanding of other subjectivities provided by the novel, for instance—this need not be an easy sentimentalism. I don't think we want to make the claim that reading *Clarissa* or *Madame Bovary* will make one behave more ethically: It might, but that claim is essentially sentimental, and sentiments are easily perverted. Indeed, the Marquis de Sade wrote his own versions of the eighteenth-century sentimental novel, gleefully twisting their educative claims. But rejecting a sentimentalist claim does not mean we cannot make a perhaps more modest but more precise claim: that the ethics of the humanities lie very much in its practices of reading, that its discipline is the discipline of close, attentive, faithful interpretive acts of reading. Getting that right can itself be an ethical act.

My understanding of what we do in the humanities brings me full circle to where we began, in Judith Butler's urgent question about how we defend the humanities and their importance in our public life without using the very language and the very framework of values that demand that we see knowledge in purely instrumental terms. This issue has gained new immediacy in the demands, registered in the United Kingdom as well as the United States, that we humanists show the deliverables of what we think and write, that we measure the impact of our research. This extends to our teaching as well. Ever since the publication of the Spellings Report (Margaret Spellings was George W. Bush's Secretary of Education) in 2006, there has been an increasing demand for a metrics to assess how much students are learning during their college education and whether college represents a cost-effective investment by parents and state agencies.[6] The problem, avers the Spellings Report, is that "parents and students have no solid evidence, comparable across institutions, of how much students learn in colleges or whether they learn more at one college than another."[7] Note the language of "how much." The solution? "Student achievement, which is inextricably connected to institutional success, must be measured by institutions on a 'value-added' basis that takes into account students' academic baseline when assessing their results. This information should be made available to students, and reported publicly in aggregate form to provide consumers and policymakers an accessible, understandable way to measure the relative effectiveness of different colleges and universities."[8] The measure of "relative effectiveness" as "value added" may remind us of the value-added tax long familiar to Europeans, which estimates the price added to a commodity on its way to market outlets.

The threat to the autonomy of universities and to academic freedom in such proposals is clear: It is a replication of No Child Left Behind on the university level, and if implemented it would have the similar result of teaching to a standard metric—indeed, teaching to tests invented to gauge that metric. I have looked at examples of the Collegiate Learning Assessment (CLA), a test recommended in the Spellings Report; the CLA is claimed to be designed to test core outcomes espoused by all of higher education—critical thinking, analytical reasoning, problem solving, and writing. The CLA has gained a fair amount of traction, is supported by some foundations, and stands to make a great deal of money if widely adopted.

The exercises on the CLA appear to test problem-solving skills. One (touted in the much-reviewed book by Richard Arum and Josipa Roksa, *Academically Adrift*) asks the student to play the role of assistant to the president of DynaTech, a company that makes precision electronic instruments and navigational equipment.[9] A member of the sales force has recommended that DynaTech purchase a small corporate plane, the SwiftAir 235, to reach customers more efficiently. But then a SwiftAir 235 crashes. The student is given a set of documents: newspaper articles about the crash, a federal accident report on in-flight breakups of single-engine planes, charts of SwiftAir's performance characteristics, an article from *Amateur Pilot* magazine comparing the 235 with competitive planes, and internal company e-mails on the proposed purchase. The student then must prepare a memo that assesses the information given and provides a recommendation as to whether DynaTech should purchase the plane.

The problem presented may resemble real-world simulations that a student would work through if he or she took a job with McKinsey Consulting. In fact, it is much like the case studies pioneered at Harvard Business School that are now considered standard in business education. It does test the student's capacity to assess data, some of it conflicting, to write a report that lays out options along with their benefits and liabilities, and to show the process by which one reaches a conclusion on the basis of the available facts and interpretations. Nonetheless, there is much that it does not test—essentially, the whole of the humanities, where the interpretation of data (that is, texts, art works, artifacts, which are often partial and incomprehensible without a deep understanding of historical, linguistic, stylistic, sociopolitical, or other context) is very different. In the humanities, interpretation is aimed not at an instrumental result (should DynaTech buy the plane?) but rather at an understanding of a past culture or the worth of a present cultural innovation. It is simply, and profoundly, a different kind of learning and knowledge.

The CLA promotes an idea that Judith Butler deplores, which has already made great inroads in our culture and our universities: that knowledge is instrumental. How do we find the language not to answer—for that would be to meet instrumentalism on its own terms—but to subvert this claim to police the field of values? Not, I think, by saying that the humanities are to be cultivated precisely because of their valuelessness. I refuse to believe that what I teach is without value. On the contrary, I think I deal with values every day. But the way in which my teaching might help my students to deal with the world is hard to specify; it surely has something to do with self-conscious reading, an ability to understand that the messages that daily claim our attention (or inattention) are created or manufactured, the productions of rhetoric rather than a natural process. I have not devised a test for the effectiveness of such teaching; but if I could concoct such a test, I think it would have to be given to the student around the time of his or her twenty-fifth reunion. It is that kind of temporal arc that I think teaching in the humanities is about.

Judith Butler at the very end of our final discussion referred the question of "measure" back to Aristotle, and I will confess that for me it is not only his *Ethics* but also his *Poetics* that offers some idea of what "measure" might mean in what I do: a treatise not about meanings but about how meanings are created, the grounds of our meaning-making acts. I hope that I teach something about that. I hope that teaching reading as a disciplined practice enables students to understand more about the human inhabitation of the world. To quote Wallace Stevens,

> From this the poem springs: that we live in a place
> That is not our own and, much more, not ourselves
> And hard it is in spite of blazoned days.[10]

That's, of course, from his *Notes toward a Supreme Fiction*. In claiming a place for the humanities in public life, we are arguing that fictions are not distractions from reality but a central means to an understanding of where and how we live in reality.

Ordinary, Incredulous

Judith Butler

We need to be more than objects of ruin.

—*Randy Martin*

I have been reflecting on the question of how best to begin this essay on humanities in the public sphere because the terms are large: humanities, the public sphere, or, perhaps more specifically, public life. Yet the sense of the task is quite precise: We have been asked to establish the relation between the two, or to provide some guidelines on how that link might be demonstrated. One reason we are asked to do this is that the link has become unsure. Certainly one of my initial responses to this invitation was simply to declare that the connection is clear. After all, we need to be able to discern what is happening in that sphere called public, to attempt to establish events and their meanings, to evaluate what we think is going on, and even to formulate modes of engagement when they are required. Can any of this happen without the capacity to read texts and images, to understand how our world is formed, and to ask what forms we want for our world, and to give reasons for preferring those forms? It would seem that all of those most basic forms of public engagement demand an education in how to read, in history, in culture and media, in philosophy and argumentation. Of course, critical thinking is a further operation of thought, which involves not taking for granted what the public sphere is.

After all, that sphere has no permanently established borders, and the borders it does have are crafted in part of the exclusion of those who are to remain unpublic, shadowed, or private. And that is surely one good reason why political engagement may be an engagement in the public sphere—but also outside it and sometimes against it. So we need to know how that public sphere has been constituted, through what media and idioms, and how it has expanded and contracted in different ways, for what reasons, and to whose benefit and whose loss. We also have to be able to evaluate the changes in the public sphere that we track.

So to ask how the humanities engage that sphere, we have to be knowing about which version of the public is at issue, how and why it works as it does, and whether it really should. Many of us have made the case for the humanities by arguing that without cultural and even public literacy it is not possible to engage as a mindful citizen in civic and democratic processes, if not more far-reaching forms of democratic struggle. We have to be able to know how to read the newspaper or understand and evaluate images in television and film, on video, and on the kiosks of the street if we are to find our way with those parts of the world that present themselves to us commonly, which does not mean they present themselves to us all in the same way. If we are to understand ourselves as not only participating in that established public sphere but engaged in the very establishing of what counts as public, then an education of the senses is required. We have to be both receptive and critical to what should be known, heard, seen, and debated within the various idioms of public life, whether they are verbal or written, visual or acoustic, architectural or haptic and performative. In this way, an education of the senses is a precondition of what we might call a sensate democracy, one in which our capacity to hear and feel is not cut short by the media on which we depend to know that world. That happens when the sphere of what can be heard, the audible and the speakable, and what can be shown, the visual and the performative, and what can be touched or neared, the conditions of mobility, are limited by any number of constraining powers. The point is not to be perfectly free to hear, speak, and show everything, or to move everywhere, but rather to evaluate the implicit limits imposed upon the senses, to track their histories and their spatial organization, and to come up with critical judgments about how the world has been organized and how it might be organized better.

What is, of course, so increasingly difficult is that we are now under pressure to describe and defend a set of propositions and beliefs that we have taken to be true, and whose value informs our daily practices and broader sense of vocation. Of course, the pressures are different whether we are at public or private institutions and depending on how elite our institutions are. But the burden is to show that engagement in public life is bound up from the start with the basics of a humanities education that address how we learn to think, to work with language and images, and to read, to make sense, to intervene, to take apart, to formulate evaluative judgments and even to make the world anew. These are such basic issues for educators that I find myself stumbling here. Must this be said, and what are the conditions under which it has become more difficult to speak and to be heard? A gap has emerged between this discourse, one that I would have thought was obvious, and a new metrics of value that is making, or has made, a claim on the obvious. Indeed, sometimes I find myself quite incredulous because I mistakenly thought the public value of these activities is so obvious that they hardly needed to be defended.[1]

I trust we all know the basic parameters of the crisis, even though we shall probably hear different versions of what it is and how it came about. Public funding for the humanities and the arts are being cut, departments of French, Italian, Russian, theatre, classics, and philosophy have been cut, or whole language departments suddenly have been merged with one another in both the United States and the United Kingdom without regard for academic concerns. Derision is sometimes publicly directed to whole domains of knowledge, including ethnic studies and critical race studies (both of which have been declared illegal in the state of Arizona), and the public value of these activities has become rapidly less than obvious. I hesitate even to give you the list of all we need to worry about because, at least in this venue, I assume that you know it. But in addition to the highly publicized closing of the French department at the State University of New York at Albany and philosophy at Middlesex in the United Kingdom, numerous other universities within the United States have cut German, Latin, Italian, and French. In 2010, it was estimated that fifty-four language programs were imperiled.[2] Now many graduate programs that used to take ten to twelve students a year have been restricted to two or even none.[3] History departments have also suffered a great deal, with clear implications for graduate education and placement. The *Chronicle of Higher Education* tells us that African history job openings fell 62 percent in 2010. Latin American history also took a large fall, down by 43 percent. The largest fields, as has been the case for years, were European and U.S. history, and even these fell by 34 and 28 percent, respectively.[4]

One can respond, "But there is a budget crisis," and either add the appellate "Stupid" or let it drift there, implied. And that has been, continues to be, true. Yet, as we know, the demand to reduce a budget or to increase revenues involves decision-making processes that invariably rely on broader schemes of values. It provides an occasion to cut programs about which doubts are raised or for which no persuasive justification is available. So if the damage done to the humanities and the arts is disproportionate, as it surely seems to be, then the question follows: What sorts of values incline administrators to decide where and what to cut? If the skepticism about the humanities (which is hardly a singular form of skepticism) informs such decisions, how does one counter that?

It was surprising for me to read the very interesting and well-researched argument by Christopher Newfield that the humanities do not constitute a drain on university finances but actually bring in the tuition that helps to fund others schools and disciplines within the university.[5] This is an interesting argument for many reasons, but perhaps most clearly because it is not always possible to establish the profitability of the discipline—its costs have to be factored through other means. But it also points to something else: Although we are clearly seeing an increasing demand to establish the profitability of disciplines, we are also seeing a new regime of values that certainly includes profitability as one component, but which includes as well "impact," marketable skills, managerial efficiency, donor appeal, the appreciation of human capital, and the internal demands of systems analysis, all of which have been identified as hallmarks of neoliberalism.[6] This set of values requires closer scrutiny as much for what it includes as for what it effaces and even pushes toward oblivion.

Pushing back against oblivion is part of my task, but I would like to prepare the way by returning to this problem of the obvious, a sense of obviousness both lost and transfigured. So here, first, is the question of when and where one register of the obvious falls away, and when and where another register comes to the fore. As I hope to suggest, understanding this kind of change may help us redirect our attention to the problem of the humanities in public life. But I will need to ask for patience as we find our way there, thus suggesting that patience remains one of the values in peril here.

If we are not sure how the humanities relate to public life, perhaps it will suffice to mark that gap between the two domains, claim that it is either a valuable difference or an inevitable one, or simply interrogate the contemporary limits of audibility within public life. Although such tactics might describe the hiatus in ways that prove interesting, they will not take us farther than a ratification of impasse nor will they precisely address our despair. One article I read about this topic asked, "How can we save that which is already dead?"[7] For that author, the fate of the humanities is tied to the fate of the university, and our energies would be better redirected toward saving the university. Though I do not deny the supervenient importance of such a task, it may be by focusing on what the humanities have to offer that we start to rethink the task of the university itself. At stake is an understanding of how the talk about a risk of death has come about, the pronouncements about a world already gone. To do this, we have to consider both the new metrics for determining value as well as the explicit forms of cultural warfare currently under way.

Although Rick Santorum exited the public arena early in the 2012 presidential race, his remarks certainly do linger and resonate in ways that remain cause for concern. They appeal to, and revel in, a thriving anti-intellectualism. His explanation for why his grades were poor at Pennsylvania State University was that his teachers were all leftists who punished him with poor grades on the basis of his political viewpoints.[8] What Santorum and those who are stoked by that sensibility regularly do is misname intellectual inquiry as itself *ideological*, where ideology refers to an adamantly held and imposed political goal, viewpoint, or framework, rather than a considered and substantiated thesis. His reference to colleges and universities as "indoctrination mills" that convert students from religion to secularism is a case in point.

Because we are briefly making lists, I propose to include the banning of more than eighty novels and books from educational use in the state of Arizona, including Matt de la Peña's *Mexican White Boy*, for containing "critical race theory," which was perversely understood as "promoting racial resentment."[9] Such arguments reduce literary works (those of Sandra Cisneros included) to imagined political viewpoints, which suggests that those who make these arguments do not really know very much about narrative voice or character, that they do not want to bother with basic questions of genre and form, and that they assume that literary narratives are transcriptions of dogma. The charge of ideology in such cases is once again coupled with a virulent anti-intellectualism.

This is important because one could be against ideology in that sense and for a more properly intellectual approach to texts—but that would be the argument of the old conservatism (which, I confess, I sometimes think I would prefer to have as my antagonist). In these instances, a form of cultural warfare has now assumed legal dimensions in some states, and it is directly linked to the devaluation and distrust of the humanities. So let us hold both these thoughts together: The politically conservative attack supplements and fortifies the managerial or neoliberal calculus that is becoming ever more dominant, but they are not, or are not always, the same trend.

Indeed, part of what has become confusing is that those who dismiss the value of the humanities often present themselves as innovators, ushering in a new age, fighting against recalcitrant and hermetic forces within the university. It is a moment, oddly, when the old-style conservatives find themselves joining with their erstwhile foes on the critical left. Those introducing some of these new metrics within public institutions of higher learning often champion new revenue enhancement schemes that will putatively save the university and they defend online education, insisting that a poetry class can be taught just as well over the Internet as around a seminar table. When some of us at the University of California at Berkeley objected to online education for such purposes, citing the importance of the practice of reading together and conducting discussions in direct reference to a text, working over the lines together, we found ourselves branded as conservative and "sentimental." So, I wonder, what has happened such that I can feel myself to be conservative within this frame of reference? It seems that different groups are now warring over the "new" and that the term has now provisionally been captured by those who seek to produce Internet-based revenue-earning programs at the expense of close reading and *learning*.

As a consequence, I, vacillating between feeling like a crazy leftist and a conservative, find myself resisting this version of the "new," noting that such proposals are slowly coming to monopolize terms such as "creative" as in "creative solutions" and even "the future." I find myself wanting to stave off a loss, one that is too great for me to bear. I even sometimes think maybe I will be lucky enough to leave the earth before I have to see the full destruction of the humanities. I note, with fear, that there are those who are willing to give up funding for the arts as "luxury items," or the humanities as a haven for leftists or as clearly useless. When the neoliberal matrix of valuation combines with the anti-intellectual conservatism, a double bind is upon us.[10] One kind of critic claims that the humanities are less than hard and profitable science and so are without value, and the other claims that the humanities deflect from the truth of religion and so are a social danger. One says there is no real world impact, and the other claims that our values have to come from "out of the pale," as it were—some anemic heavenly elsewhere that inscribes our values and our laws.

What I assume to be a common understanding seems increasingly elusive. The obvious should be that to which we merely need to point to recall to ourselves its status. Yet what happens when what we have considered obvious becomes obscure, or when possibilities thought too obscure slowly become installed as obvious? It is not enough to be astonished or outraged because that does not translate into a way to reestablish a different sense of reality, a different register of the obvious. However, if we feel no astonishment or outrage, we have become inured to the attack itself, acquiescent or complicitous, effectively recruited into the project of accepting this new sense of the obvious, this sense of the obvious that now, eerily, lays claim to the new.

Of course, one can see that I am already on a certain theoretical terrain, for what does it mean that different versions of the obvious can be achieved or lost? It is not enough to say, for instance, that some version of the obvious has become dominant. If it is dominant, then there are rival understandings, however marginal, and so the version of reality we are discussing may be trying to achieve dominance but has not. The word *ideology* links with the problem of the obvious here. Of course, there are those who think that universities have become ideological and that the humanities are their ideological center; yet this position reflexively disqualifies itself, for its own position becomes an ideological attack on the humanities from the opposite side of the political spectrum, which is just a way of saying that it is all war. This view is finally unproductive if we seek to understand what is meant by ideology and whether it has a place in these debates.

Louis Althusser once sought to account for the ideological surface of things as "the obvious" and spent some time trying to fathom how the obvious gets established as such.[11] He was, of course, talking about the relationship between the State and the facts of oppression, and what emerges from this relationship is what he called "a very special kind of obviousness."[12] Indeed, in his language, no one person or subject makes this happen, but the relationship between the State and its subjects gives rise to this special kind of obviousness as a feature of their rapport. He gives us the propositional form of this obviousness: "Yes, that's how it is, that's really true!"[13] Our ability to grasp Althusser's concept of ideology depends first on seeing how the one who utters these lines is related to the one who hears these lines. Because the voice appears in a written text, it follows that writing and reading become essential to a critical understanding of what he calls ideology; in fact, ideology is not just a system of thought, but constitutes us in relation to one another as the reading and writing subjects we are. Ideology does not induce our existence or cause us to be; rather, it emerges as a way of describing that web of relations that tethers authors and readers: In his words, "both live 'spontaneously' or 'naturally' in ideology."[14] So he describes the medium in which we live, one that is populated by readers and writers, but surely also by speakers and listeners—those appearing and seen, those moving or still in relation to others who are negotiating mobility as well. We live "in" ideology as we might live in a certain climate; indeed, it is a climate of historical belief with the proviso that it is not precisely *we* who manufacture and hold to a set of beliefs, but rather a set of beliefs breezes through us, animating the exchange of thought. So ideology is not precisely what a critic takes apart or gets beyond at a moment's notice; it is rather more like an ethos in which we converge, if not the cultural surface that supports our gravity and mobility. This does not mean an ideology is always singular and cannot shift and change, as sometimes the obviousness on which it relies fissures, and that opening cannot be readily closed.

One might expect that the name of Althusser would be among those authors that Santorum is worried about (if, that is, it can be shown that Santorum knows about Althusser, which seems unlikely). Althusser might be required reading for the "indoctrination mill" that converts religious believers into secularists. My suggestion is that it turns out that belief is quite important to Althusser's conception of ideology, as is the institution of the Church and its scriptures; in my view, it is not so easy to brand him a Marxist secularist because the form of belief he names ideological is not simply overcome or negated with a well-reasoned critique of its operation. Trying to explain this sense of obviousness that tethers us as readers and writers, Althusser sought recourse to Saint Paul. In his words, "As St Paul admirably put it, it is in the 'Logos', meaning in ideology, that we 'live, move and have our being'."[15] Saint Paul is already describing ideology, and in that way making a contribution to Marxist theory *avant la lettre*. Immediately then, Althusser concludes, "It follows that, for you and for me, the category of the subject is a primary 'obviousness' (obviousnesses are always primary): it is clear that you and I are subjects (free, ethical, etc. . . .). Like all obviousnesses, including those that make a word 'name a thing' or 'have a meaning' (therefore including the obviousness of the 'transparency' of language)." In some nonobvious, nonapparent way, what Althusser calls ideology imposes "obviousnesses as obviousnesses."[16] At this point, a rather nonobvious, if perfectly obscure, use of language seems to emerge, because we are not used to that plural noun form "obviousnesses." I even worry about stating it out loud because it could easily be used as grist for the mill—not the indoctrination mill, but the one that seeks to grind up the humanities for having experimented with language in ways that seem obscure, if not frivolous.

Still, when something is being established as obvious to us through a process of some kind, it surely takes place in a nonobvious sort of way, if not in an utterly obscure one. Obscurity names the process by which the obvious is established. When something is being made less than obvious, obscurity emerges, but the terms are clearly relative. For Althusser, an obviousness is that which we "cannot fail to recognize"; and we, as subjects, are defined in part by what he calls the "ritual practice of ideological recognition in everyday life."[17] We have friends, he tells us, who knock on the door, and when we ask, "Who's there?" they reply "It's me," and at that moment of exchange we recognize that person as the friend we know. With some reflection, we understand that all sorts of "mes" say "it's me" when someone asks, "who's there?," and so it could be any number of "mes" who are in fact calling or knocking at that instant. Despite the non-singularity of my response, the singular me is sometimes recognized: "Oh, it's you." This happens between authors and writers, and between speakers and their audiences. Althusser then breaks out into reflexivity: "The writing I am currently executing and the reading you are currently performing are also in this respect rituals of ideological recognition, including the 'obviousness' with which the 'truth' or 'error' of my reflections may impose itself on you."[18]

Take this example from Franz Kafka's "Description of a Struggle," a story he wrote in 1904 and completed about five years later.[19] He is writing, we might say, in a world or in a climate where certain kinds of obvious realities are vanishing or where their episodic reappearance is no less than astonishing. It is a story that includes a scene in which two men encounter each other in church, but neither of them is able quite to stand up or balance with ease. The one moves his leg as one would move a prosthesis, though he is not wearing one. The other seeks to balance himself in ways that can only produce imbalance. They lunge awkwardly at one another in vain attempts at communication. The one leans back impossibly, and the other bows down near the other in ways that are both potentially sexual and utterly uncomfortable. The first-person narrator notes that he is no longer able to walk in an upright way, that normal steps elude him. He asks, "Am I not rather entitled to complain bitterly at having to skip along the houses like a shadow without a clear outline, sometimes disappearing in the panes of the shopwindows?" He continues, "Oh, what dreadful days I have to live through! Why is everything so badly built that high houses collapse every now and again for no apparent reason? On these occasions I clamber over the rubble, asking everyone I meet: 'How could this have happened?' In our town—a new house—how many does that make today?—Just think of it!' And no one can give me an answer."[20] So what should be established and built becomes undone with surprising speed, leaving in its wake a sense that the spatial and temporal coordinates of the world do not hold, or rather no longer hold, or rather never did.

What follows is a description of everyday life that has gone awry, where what is most obvious seems to become most obscure. The narrator continues, "Frequently people fall in the street and lie there dead. Whereupon all the shop people open their doors laden with wares, hurry busily out, cart the dead into a house, come out again all smiles, then the chatter begins: 'Good Morning—it's a dull day—I'm selling any amount of kerchiefs—ah yes, the war.' I rush into the house, and after raising my hand several times timidly with my finger crooked, I finally knock on the janitor's little window: 'Good morning,' I say, 'I understand a dead man was carried in here just now.'" Then, after some pausing and a failed effort on the part of the narrator to pass himself off as secret police, the man replies, "'There's no dead man here. Maybe next door.' I raise my hat and go."[21]

After such a moment, the body does not hold together, and gravity is altogether lost. A sharp wind rises, and the narrator looks up at a church where "the Virgin Mary's cloak is coiling around her pillar and the wind is tugging at it. Does no one notice this? The ladies and gentlemen who should be walking on the pavement are floating. When the wind falls they stand still, say a few words, and bow to one another, but when the wind rises again they are helpless, and all their feet leave the ground at the same time."[22] And then, in a transition that seems like a non sequitur, the listener replies, bringing us back to that vanishing sense of the obvious with which we are concerned. He recalls an earlier moment in their exchange where the narrator asks, "Why is it that around me things sink away like fallen snow, whereas for other people even a little liqueur glass stands on the table steady as a statue?" Then, "So, you don't believe this happens to other people? You really don't? Just listen, then. When as a child I opened my eyes after a brief afternoon nap, still not quite sure I was alive, I heard my mother up on the balcony asking in a natural tone of voice: 'What are you doing my dear? Goodness, isn't it hot?' From the garden a woman answered, 'Me, I'm having my tea on the lawn.' They spoke casually and not very distinctly, as though this woman had expected the question, my mother the answer."[23]

"Me, I'm having my tea on the lawn"—the reply, a moment in which the woman simply refers to what she is doing and offers up that information to someone listening, certainly gives rise to a sense of obviousness,

surely analogous to "Who's there?" "It's me." This very exchange, however, is cited within another conversation, and in that new conversation,
the old conversation is cause for astonishment and doubt. Later in the
story, after the description of the buildings falling and the dead bodies
whisked away inside of shops where the shopkeepers deny their existence,
this simple story about having tea on the lawn is recalled. The one listening replies, "'That story you told me earlier about your mother and the
woman in the garden I really don't find so remarkable. Not only have I
heard and experienced many stories of this kind, I have even taken part in
some. The whole thing is perfectly natural. Do you really mean to suggest
that had I been on that balcony in the summer, I could not have asked the
same question and given the same answer from the garden? Quite an
ordinary occurrence!'"[24] That last claim is only slightly belied by the
exclamation mark by which it ends, suggesting that the ordinary emphati-
cally seeks to counter a sense of the vanishing ordinary.

The whole exchange ends with the one who narrated the reported
exchange between the mother and the woman in the garden feeling very
much relieved, suddenly engaging in perfectly ordinary discourse, com-
menting on the other's tie, how well dressed he is, as if the two are conse-
crating the ordinary. Like those who quickly forget that there were dead
bodies on the street and now engage in small talk about the weather, the
narrator clings to the daily discourse of chatter and compliments. Although
the story was written in 1904, a decade before World War I, Kafka's way of
registering ineffable events such as these proved prescient. On August 2,
1914, he wrote in his diary, "Germany declares war on Russia—in the afternoon, swimming lessons."[25]

In the sudden recourse to the ordinary and obvious has something
thereby been resolved, or has something just been covered over? The final
line of that section then arrives: "confessions became most comprehensible when they were retracted."[26] It is a paradoxical line, but perhaps not
altogether confusing. After all, what is comprehensible is not precisely the
ordinary exchange, the polite discourse, the everyday compliments; they
cover over and defer a sense of the world that is losing its stability, pulled
into oblivion. The wind that lifts those bodies up in the air, disrupts conversations, exposes the dead on the street, and unleashes fear might be
understood as the particular climate of the obvious in which Kafka's characters move and live. At one point when the pedestrians are lifted off the
pavement, they hold onto their hats, and "'their eyes twinkle gaily enough
and no one has the slightest fault to find with the weather.'" The paragraph
ends, "'I'm the only one who's afraid.'"[27]

I noted earlier that we could mark the hiatus between the emerging metrics of value and those that belong to the humanities, but that would not be enough to redirect our actions or to remake the world. Yet this gap within the obvious that Kafka's writings opens up creates an ethical possibility. Exposing this very gap between what has become ordinary and the destructive aims it covers over and conveys, the reader is propelled into ethical responsiveness and alert. In Althusser, it seems that ideology names the effective functioning of the ordinary, in which when I knock, the "me" is then recognized—that is, when a simple act of saying what one is doing is received by another and understood. It is me, knocking at the door. Yes, you, glad to see you again. Me, I am having my tea on the lawn. There is a ground on which I might rest, a simple act of drinking, an ability to refer to myself and to say to you what it is I am doing. The basics of gravity, world, nourishment, and communication are intact for those brief episodes.

Yet Kafka's story queries the conditions under which the solidity of the world and the possibility of exchange have slipped away or are currently slipping. Kafka's texts tend to relay events in neutral and observational narrative voices (various "reports" and "investigations" refine the tenor of the bureaucratic voice). When scenes of outrage, destruction, and suffering are relayed through such a narrative voice, a gap opens between the mode of presentation and what is presented; the reader not only sees the outrage, but feels the ease with which outrage is normalized and covered over. A fissure emerges within the discourse of the obvious that shows the obscure workings of those modes of voice and discourse that cover over frightening and unacceptable destruction and loss. The narrative voice actually does the covering over of such outrages at the same time that it gives us the distance to respond to, and evaluate, that state of affairs.

As we read, we are brought into the mechanisms by which those dead bodies on the street are whisked away and the dissimulating function of daily chatter, and they prove to be unlivable. As we read those voices, as they depart from one another and converge again, we enact the ideological in Althusser's terms, but we also are given reason for alarm, and we cannot turn away from what has just been shown. The point is not to engender shock and outrage without any further recourse to action. Rather, we are compelled to understand the loss of communication as the new obvious, the sudden vanishing of the image of suffering; the cover up through a neutralized and cheery discourse of devastations induces incredulity—is incredible, if not incredulous—exceeding the syntax that keeps it in place: the ordinary incredulous. The writing steeps us in the process of making and unmaking a world, which is not to say that the world is made through writing.

One could be tempted simply to say that we must gather the strength to defend the obvious. Alain Badiou does this when he cites Wallace Stevens's poem "Man Carrying Thing": "the bright obvious will stand motionless."[28] I am less convinced that the line from Stevens is without irony, but I can see why those who wish to retrench Plato would read it as Badiou does. My suggestion is that if Kafka can be read together with Althusser, one place where the obvious and its unraveling occurs is in reading and writing, in all the modes of exchange, visual, oral, and haptic, in which we are relatively tethered to one another. To rethink the problem of the ideological in Kafka's terms, we might begin by asking whether the very basic propositions about speaking and listening, reading and writing, showing and seeing, have become undone, unleashing astonishment and fear, alerting us as well to what has been destroyed, what might yet be destroyed, and what it would mean to preserve and reanimate what is most valuable.

In the final section of this essay, then, let me consider some of the salient forms that the defense of the humanities has taken and elaborate on what I think of as the ethical task before us, one that is, in my view, indissociable from forms of critical judgment and what we might aptly call the struggle against oblivion. My point will not be that we need to refine our skills of critical dismantling, but rather I wish to link our critical practice to an ethical consideration of the forms of cultural aliveness and destruction for which we are compelled to struggle because they are linked with public questions of what is of value, and what should be.

In the past few years, I have heard and read several kinds of arguments about how best to defend the humanities. Here is a brief list: the humanities have intrinsic value; the humanities are useless, and that is their value; public intellectuals exemplify the value of the humanities for public life; the humanities offer certain kinds of skill development that are important for economic mobility; the humanities offer certain kinds of literacy that are indispensable to citizenship; and finally, the humanities offer a critical perspective on values that can actively engage the contemporary metrics of value by which the humanities themselves are weakened, if not destroyed.

Some of my colleagues claim that the humanities must be recognized for having the "intrinsic value" that they have. Of course, the problem emerges that others do not recognize that intrinsic value—at which point, the intrinsic value must be demonstrated. If it must be demonstrated, it has to be demonstrated within a language and an idiom that can be recognized by those who most clearly need to be convinced of that value. And that language is, increasingly, one that cannot recognize the value of the humanities, or can recognize it only with difficulty, because the kinds of values recognized by such a language, that are registered in that language, are those that cover over or consign to oblivion the value of the humanities.

The defense of intrinsic value has a close cousin in the position that the humanities are useless and should be defended as useless. For some, the humanities are themselves based on a critique of instrumentality, and they form the institutional venue for the critique of utility, functionalism, and instrumentality more generally. Theodor Adorno, for instance, had this to say about poetry: "The lyric reveals itself to be most deeply grounded in society when it does not chime in with society, *when it communicates nothing*."[29] For Adorno, to communicate nothing is precisely to refuse the structures of communication that ratify society, and so the most "critical" potential of the lyric is expressed when communication is refused. For Kafka, the loss of communication is minimally twofold: Its loss is mourned at the same time that its capacity to consign matters of life and death to oblivion, horrifying, sounds an ethical alarm.

Yet others point to the idea of the public intellectual or to examples of public intellectuals, or find in literary works examples of virtuous people or citizens we should try to emulate. In my view, in thinking about the humanities and the public sphere, we need to move beyond the idea of the public intellectual to a broader reflection on the humanities in the public sphere.[30] The time for showcasing exemplary public intellectuals is probably gone—although some administrators and grant officers are eager to fund "leadership" proposals that allow exemplary individuals to be separated off and rewarded at the expense of funding institutional infrastructures or supplementing fellowships for students with limited financial means.

Another claim is that we must develop skills in our students that can be demonstrated to be useful for economic life or indispensable for public life and citizenship, more specifically. If we produce or instill skills, then we can show how skills can be used and implemented, which gives us recourse to a practical dimension. Strong defenders of the humanities take some version of this position. Geoffrey Harpham, for instance, writes that "we cannot simply insist that knowledge is only worthy of the name if it is pursued for its own sake, and that liberal education is contaminated when subjected to utilitarian justifications."[31] That seems to imply that we must adapt what we do to contemporary measures of instrumentality, or that we must find some way of translating between what we do and those particular metrics of value. In any case, we cannot afford to continue to understand our vocation as a form of purity.

I agree that the arguments of intrinsic value or uselessness do not suffice (though some of my heartstrings, I confess, are pulled by both). But still, we have to ask: If the humanities are to make a difference in public life, does that mean we have to say that they are instrumental to some other social good? Is instrumentality the only way we have of thinking about what it means to make a difference? Indeed, we are faced with new metrics and standards of evaluation, and some of them are rather disorienting for those who have worked for a lifetime within the humanities. Interestingly, not all ways of "making a difference" count as having a calculable impact, according to these new metrics. A colleague in the United Kingdom proposed a conference for funding from their Arts and Humanities Research Council that would focus on the various meanings of monarchy for European countries at the present time. The proposal was rejected, and the reason given was that it failed to demonstrate "impact." When she queried what "impact" might mean for such a conference, the grant administrators said that she would have to show that the findings of any such conference would be applicable to contemporary policy; indeed, their Web site explicitly states that "impact" refers to the "demonstrable contribution that excellent research makes to society and the economy," and adds that "contribution" can be gauged by demonstrating how the knowledge generated can be "transferred" to individuals and communities outside of the academy. Her response was to suggest that the conference might help bring about the downfall of the monarchy, but her potential funders were not amused, and the project failed. Yet what other result would have fulfilled their requirement? Oddly, for her to have provided impact under such a circumstance would have immediately made her available for another sort of criticism, namely, that scholarship has been skewed by ideological aims, especially of the left-wing sort that are regularly associated with the humanities both in the United Kingdom and the United States—without, I would add, good grounds for doing so.

Of course, I want to say, and do say, that the humanities matter. But as soon as we say that, we have to show what we mean by mattering, and that is where we get into a set of disagreements that are both difficult and invaluable. If we take Harpham's point to mean that we have to adopt instrumentality as the measure of value, then we have accepted that particular scheme of evaluation as the most relevant and appropriate. But I think what he is claiming is that we cannot avoid considerations of instrumentality altogether. Here is the bind: We may well think that we must conform to the standards implied by the demands themselves in order to offer a satisfactory answer and receive the funding we need, whether those are internal allocations, revenue from investments, government grants, the largesse of private donors, or the budget lines from state assemblies if we are in public institutions. Yet if we comply too well—that is, too perfectly—we run the risk of forfeiting one of the most important tasks of the humanities, namely, to think critically about modes of measurement and schemes of evaluation in order to figure out which ones are justified, which ones really suit their objects, and which ones are introduced and maintained by the scholarship and teaching in the humanities. This process of thinking critically involves reading closely the various public documents that are deciding our fate while also exercising a particular kind of judgment as we read. As I hope to suggest, this exercise of critical judgment also establishes an important link between the humanities and public life.

We also could call this the critical problem of value. If there are competing ways of measuring value or making evaluations—some of which argue explicitly that value cannot be measured, or minimally that not all kinds of value can be measured—then how do we begin to adjudicate that situation? The humanities are under pressure to demonstrate their value under historical conditions in which competing schemes of valuation are brought to bear upon the humanities. We can simply conform to the ones that look most lucrative, at which point we may well be able to fund the humanities, until it becomes clear that we do not actually do what we said we were going to do in order to get the funding we need. "We have funding for the humanities! The humanities are lost." But even if we decide that, tactically, that is the only way to go, we compel the humanities to conform to models that misrecognize or even efface their value, at which point we have to ask what we are actually funding, and at what cost, and how it relates to the ideal we want to preserve and animate.

Critical judgment implies an investigation of the problem of value, something that is a problem precisely because values are plural and do not always complement one another. In the second instance, that form of critical judgment implies finding ways to evaluate disparate schemes of valuation, that is, asking about which schemes are best for the humanities and how might we demonstrate that persuasively. When ideas of instrumentality, impact, skill building, and revenue enhancement become the dominant modes of evaluation, then certain managerial, financial, and more broadly neoliberal modes of valuation gain ascendancy. It then remains for some group of interested educators to query whether those schemes are finally sufficient, and whether the humanities can even successfully make a case for itself in the terms required by those schemes. One could become a realist under such conditions and argue that we have no other choice: We must make those arguments and in those terms. Or one could become a purist and say that we will never make those arguments within those terms. But no matter which way we go, we are still left with a problem of knowledge that needs to be foregrounded and safeguarded, namely, the very practice of asking about *the value* of these values, whether they are comprehensive, what they facilitate, what they foreclose, what kind of world they establish, and what kind of world they destroy.

How does this issue of critical judgment bring us to the question of how the humanities link up with public life—more particularly, the relation between the humanities and citizenship or, more broadly, the forms of democratic engagement? The meaning of citizenship, if it is to be valuable for our purposes, must describe a set of practices that can be undertaken by the documented and the undocumented. So citizenship has to belong to those who are not legally stipulated as citizens. Citizenship is thus a topic for public debate, which means that established stipulations on citizenship cannot be equated from the public sphere. Indeed, the public sphere can be a place where the noncitizen feels endangered or exercises rights that are not guaranteed by any existing form of citizenship. Sequestered within the public sphere, the undocumented expose the limits of using citizenship to define the public.

We can begin with some of the prerogatives of citizenship to find our way into this larger question. We have reason to doubt whether democracy is possible at all without an educated public, and to wonder what forms of education are necessary for democracy to work. Here it seems important to note, as Wendy Brown has argued, that as public and affordable higher education becomes out of reach for the poor and the working class, new class hierarchies emerge such that the monied not only get more education but also gain access to more prestigious institutions and greater upward mobility, protecting their already upward trajectory.[32] Although this surely counts as an "instrumental" argument for increasing educational opportunities for those who cannot afford them, there is another argument that is implicit in this one. Brown remarks that citizens have to deliberate on how best to make a world together, and this requires that they are able to reflect on how they themselves have been formed, especially on the political formations that have brought them to where they are, to the views they hold. They also need to be able deliberate together on how best to organize their world, and this means working together on the question of where to find or make ideals, how best to evaluate them, and how to make a world that might either realize those ideals or keep them alive as possibilities. Dana Villa said something similar in his book, *Socratic Citizenship*, when, drawing on Arendt and Socrates, he argued that only through a common reflection on the world do we begin to exercise judgment as individuals who are bound with others.[33]

As you can see, the living scene of the seminar, or reading and writing and disputation, is in some ways related to the practice of citizenship, often a conflicted process that requires forms of interpretation, deliberation, and the setting forth of ideals. But it can also be that the practice of interpretation leads us to say no to an entire regime, to refuse it, to counter it, and to demand a new way of ordering the world. The analogy with citizenship breaks down, however, when we consider that sometimes reading can take us to an insight into the necessary limits of a regime, especially when we see the losses it induces and refuses to mourn. This might imply undoing forms of public engagement that exceed the existing forms of citizenship, or even calling for their remaking. And when we arrive there, or when we defend that practice of calling into question whether a regime should continue as it is, we are exercising a form of judgment that is precisely not valorized by the regime itself. This form of evaluating is not just about bringing something down because it is unjust or because its consequences are destructive in ways that cannot be ethically abided, it is a bringing down and bringing forth; it is thus the condition, we might say, of both revolution and critical judgment.

The point is not only to reflect on the history that makes our present world possible, or the various forms that bespeak and ratify our contemporary modes of valuation, but to figure out in common what we make of it and what we want to make of it. If we are presented with a debate, for instance, in which we have to show that the humanities can have a larger impact or that the humanities can be profitable, and we are asked to choose between them, this is surely a moment for pausing, refusing, and offering another perspective. Socially and politically, we are in a bind because the imperative to "save" the humanities often propels us into states of urgency in which we imagine that the only future left to us will be one secured precisely through those metrics of value that are most in need of critical re-evaluation. Oddly, our very capacity for critically re-evaluating is what cannot be measured by the metrics by which the humanities are increasingly judged. This means that the resource we need to save the humanities is precisely one that has been abandoned by the metrics that promise to save the humanities if only we comply. So perhaps we must retrieve from the threat of oblivion those ways of valuing that can put into perspective the closing of the horizons enacted by the metrics we are asked to use. These are metrics of forgetfulness, perhaps, or metrics of effacement, conduits to oblivion, where the calculus emerges as the final arbiter of value, which means that the values we have to defend are already lost. This does not mean that we become conservative, endeavoring to reinstate a former time; rather, we must move forward in new ways, through new idioms, and with some impurity, to reanimate the very ideals that guide and justify our work.

Here, one can see how easy it is to resolve upon mourning or to rise up in impotent outrage and refuse to go gently into that dark night. But is there a politics that fights against the pull of oblivion? Let me end with an example that perhaps makes my point in a way that I hope will not prove to be too obscure. But if obscurity is sometimes the necessary corrective to what has become obvious, so be it.

I was asked to help devise a proposal to have an institute funded that would be, ironically, dedicated to the problem of values. One of the grant administrators let me know that I would have to be able to show "the deliverable." I asked whether this was really a word, and she replied that it surely was, and offered me a definition from a Web site called *Investopedia*.[34] Here is that definition:

> Deliverable: "a project management term for the quantifiable goods or services that will be provided upon completion of a project. Deliverables can be tangible or intangible parts of the developmental process, and are often specified functions or characteristics of the project."

The Web site, by way of offering a further explanation, continued:

> Deliverables serves as a general term that encompasses the requirements of a project. A deliverable may be an object, used in the greater scheme of the project. For example, in a project meant to upgrade a firm's technology, a deliverable may be a dozen new computers. Alternatively, a deliverable may be a function or an aspect of the overall project. For example, a software project may have a deliverable specifying that the

computer program must be able to compute a company's accounts receivable.

Actually, the question posed to me did not distinguish between singular and plural forms of the deliverable. It was simply "What is the deliverable of your proposal?" As I scrutinized the word, I thought first that a deliverable must be different from a delivery, or something that can be delivered, such as a package or a gift, a kiss, a legal summons, or a swift punch to the jaw. The deliverable seemed to be a noun form that seeks to make a concrete thing out of the very possibility of a delivery. In other words, the term seemed to refer to what *can* be delivered, what it is possible to deliver. For me, this immediately brought up questions of theology and semiotics alike, though I can imagine also situations of love and bribery that center on the idea of what can be delivered. There is surely a question of whether, for instance, God's word has been delivered, can be delivered, will ever yet be delivered. There is also a question about human communication: Is it possible to send a letter that will be delivered, and delivered in a sense that means that the letter arrives at its destination and is received or read? (This is the problematic of Kafka's "An Imperial Message.") The delivery of a letter or the delivery of God's word both seem to depend on a form of communication that works, that is, where what is sent and what is delivered turn out to be the same, or, at least, where what is sent can become what is delivered through some set of relays, technologies, transpositions, or translations.

It interests me that the *Investopedia* clarification of the term distinguishes between tangible and intangible forms of the deliverable. I find myself eagerly anticipating the intangible. But when it then gives examples of the two, the tangible seems to be "new computers" and the intangible seems to be "the ability to compute a company's accounts receivable." The line that seeks to explain the deliverable ends with the word "receivable," at which point my attention as a literary reader started to flare. We do talk about "receivables" when we talk about accounts, and in some way the receivable is implied by the deliverable. If we do not deliver, we will not receive. But even that formulation does not quite capture what is at play, because the term is concerned less with what *is delivered* than with what *can be delivered*, and what *can be received*. These are potentialities of a process, and they are given a noun form.

There is an odd resonance with what some of us do. When I pose a question, after reading Kafka, for instance, such as "whose lives are grievable and whose lives are recognizable under conditions of war?," an editor usually comes back to me with the suggestion that I simply ask whose lives are worthy of grief, and whose lives can be recognized. I balk a little because I want to draw attention to a quality that gets lost in that simpler formulation. I want to say that sometimes people seem to be endowed with a certain value, that is, their lives are regarded as valuable and they assume a certain form and bearing under that regard. Great efforts are made to protect and defend those lives, and yet in other instances, lives are regarded as disposable or are so stripped of value that when they are imperiled, injured, or lost, they assume a social ontology that is partially constituted by that regard. Hence, they are not cause for worry; their potential loss is no occasion to mourn. Someone who never existed has been nullified, so nothing has happened. The "grievable" postulates a future conditional, a perspective from the future; indeed, to be grievable is a precondition of being valuable in the present: If there were a war or a disaster, some populations would be designated as worthy of grief whereas others would not. As a way of conjecturing, even fictionalizing, that adjectival noun seeks to bring to bear the ethical relation to a future loss on the thinking of the present. I suppose the conjectured temporality implied by such a noun-adjective is not unlike the way that utopian fictions sometimes establish an imaginary future perspective from which critical light can be shed on the inequalities and injustices of the contemporary organization of society. It is also necessary for what Ernst Bloch once called the principle of hope.[35]

I mean to say that a certain group of people considered grievable could be mourned if they were lost, and so carry that quality in the present; in contrast, the ungrievable bear the mark of those who will never be mourned because they were never understood to be living. So what does this have to do with the deliverable? When am I going to deliver? Is this essay finally deliverable? We might ask of the deliverable: Does it also sustain a relation to the future and, if so, what kind? If something is a deliverable, it does not have to be actually delivered to sustain that quality. It has only to be an object or a function or an aspect of a project that could be delivered, if certain conditions were to be met. Indeed, in the context of the grant application, the deliverable can become the delivered only on the condition that the project is funded and then executed.

If "receivable" belongs to the world of accounts, then the deliverable belongs to the prior world in which the receivable is anticipated. These are aspects of a process and a project, and certain questions cannot rightly be asked of this framework: who delivers, what do they deliver, and who receives, if anyone does? What is undeliverable, or deemed undeliverable by this process? In other words, who loses, and what is lost?

Such terms contain a futural or even transcendent function, and perhaps we can read them as recirculating in fugitive forms the traces or remnants of a theology and a semiotics that belong precisely to the domain that is no longer recognizable within their terms. For the deliverable is the possibility opened up by the project, a way of organizing and regulating time, constraining the future. After all, the deliverable refers to the general conditions of delivery, and so is something that transcends every particular delivery, every particular package, every particular fund that is actually received in any particular account in payment for what is delivered. Perhaps the deliverable is thus the ruin and remnant of Platonism; perhaps, it is the perversely animated trace of transcendence, a new obviousnessness that carries and condenses the no longer translatable form of the humanities within a single word, adding insult to injury by virtue of being a very bad kind of poetry. It puts out of play any question of what can be received or should be received, any question of who stands to receive or who stands to lose, questions that pertain to distributive justice; it sets aside questions of what values it preempts, and what values it installs as the new obvious.

Perhaps this strangely condensed noun gives off a peculiar illumination that belongs to our time, opening a future that is bound precisely through a discourse that consigns to oblivion some of the questions that are most valuable. The deliverable might be said to displace and efface the history of value that it is meant to gauge. In this way, we can perhaps conclude that the deliverable produces the ungrievable, absorbing and renaming the trace of loss so that we are no longer able to stay with the thought of those bodies on the street or more broadly the question of what we undergo, whether it is just, and what new forms of life we have yet to make.

So if we return to where we began, with the question of how practitioners of the humanities can be more than or other than the objects of ruin, we now have a slightly different path. We find ourselves housed and displaced within language with metrics of value that not only cannot gauge well what we do, but have so monopolized the field of value that they threaten to consign what we do to oblivion. What can those whose language is consigned to oblivion do? They can reenter the fray, open up the space between the language that has become obvious or self-evident and the enormous loss it has already accomplished and still portends. That gap is the advent of an ethical relation not only to the past and the future but to the possibility of incredulity and astonishment when the value of the new regime of values has yet to be evaluated. This means that we exercise critical judgment in the breach, reentering the obscure into the obvious in order to affirm what is left between us still to lose, to keep, to keep animated. In this way, we militate for a sphere of audibility within which to pose our question and have it heard: What now is the value of our values?

I

Is There an Ethics of Reading?

Poetry, Injury, and the Ethics of Reading

Elaine Scarry

What is the ethical power of literature? Can it diminish acts of injuring, and if it can, what aspects of literature deserve the credit?

All these questions, at first, hinge on another: Can *anything* diminish injury? In his book *The Better Angels of Our Nature*, Steven Pinker argues that, over 50 centuries, many forms of violence have subsided.[1] Among the epochs he singles out for special scrutiny is a hundred-year period bridging the seventeenth and eighteenth centuries during which an array of brutal acts—executing accused witches, imprisoning debtors, torturing animals, torturing humans, inflicting the death penalty, enslaving fellow human beings—suddenly abated, even if they did not disappear.

Attempting to account for "the sweeping change in everyday sensibilities" toward "the suffering in other living things" and for the protective laws that emerged during the Humanitarian Revolution, Pinker argues that the legal reforms were in some degree a product of increasing literacy. Reforms were immediately preceded by a startling increase in book production (for example, in England, the number of publications rose from fewer than 500 per decade in 1600 to 2,000 per decade by 1700, and 7,000 per decade by 1800[2]) and by an equally startling surge in literacy, with the majority of Englishmen literate by the end of the seventeenth century, the French by the end of the eighteenth century, and the Danish, Finnish, German, Icelandic, Scottish, Swedish, and Swiss by the end of the nineteenth century.[3]

Pinker singles out one particular form of reading and one particular kind of book, the novel—though, as we will see, features of poetry that long predate the novels of this period are essential to literature's capacity to reduce harm. Drawing elaborately on the work of historian Lynn Hunt, Pinker convincingly describes the effect of men reading best-selling novels such as Richardson's *Pamela* and Rousseau's *Julie* and thereby entering imaginatively into the lives of other people, including those without social power: women, servants, and children.[4] Pinker gives a picture of human mental life before and after the literacy revolution: "The pokey little world of village and clan, accessible through the five senses and informed by a single content provider, the church, gave way to a phantasmagoria of people, places, cultures, and ideas."[5]

If we assume (on the basis of very incomplete evidence) that literature has in fact helped to diminish acts of injuring—not only during the Humanitarian Revolution, but also in other epochs—what attributes of literature can explain this? Three come immediately to mind: its invitation to empathy, its reliance on deliberative thought, and its beauty.

Because empathy is so fundamental to literature, it has been defended, doubted, berated, and celebrated countless times. Though it deserves to be examined countless times more, I will not dedicate space to it here except to note the following: By "empathy," Hunt and Pinker—rightly in my view—mean not the capacity of literature to make us feel compassion for a fictional being (though literature certainly does this), but rather the capacity of literature to exercise and reinforce our recognition that there *are* other points of view in the world, and to make this recognition a powerful mental habit. If this recognition occurs in a large enough population, then a law against injuring others can be passed, after which the prohibition it expresses becomes freestanding and independent of sensibility.[6] Literature says, "Imagine Pamela, and her right to be free of injury will become self-evident to you." The laws say, "We are not interested in your imaginative abilities or disabilities; whether or not you can imagine Pamela, you are prohibited from injuring her."

The novel's capacity to evoke readers' empathy has antecedents. It was anticipated by the second attribute of literature that works against injury: the deliberative push embedded in poetry.

The connection of poetic composition to deliberation—to the "pro" and "con" of debate—is in the very first description we have of the muses singing, the one Homer gives at the close of the first book of the *Iliad*. Thomas Hobbes, who was acutely interested in deliberation, wrote in his 1676 translation, beginning with the feasting of the gods, "And all the day from morning unto night / Ambrosia they eat, and nectar drink. / Apollo played, and alternately / The Muses to him sung." The alternating voices of the Muses are audible in Alexander Pope's later translation, as in John Ogilby's earlier one.[7] Ogilby's annotation to the lines states: "The Muses sung in course answering one the other . . . Anthem-wise; [the Greek Homer uses] being such Orations as were made *pro* and *con* upon the same argument."[8] He then invokes Virgil's *Eclogue*, "The Muses always lov'd alternate Verse," and Hesiod's *Theogony*, "Muses begin, and Muses end the Song." The argumentative structure enacted by Homer's Muses is registered in every English translation, with the exception of George Chapman's. Samuel Butler writes, "The Muses lifted up their sweet voices, calling and answering to one another"; in Richmond Lattimore's edition, we read of the "antiphonal sweet sound of the Muses singing"; and Robert Fagles has the "Muses singing / voice to voice in chorus."[9]

The *Iliad* is an epic ignited by the dispute between Achilles and Agamemnon, and we are more likely to associate dispute with epic poetry or with plays, as in the drama contests of fifth-century Greece. But many other genres of poetry have the debate structure built into them, as we can see by the word "anthem"—derived from "antiphone" or "verse response"—which surfaces in the translations. That an anthem, or hymn of praise, holds disputing voice within it reminds us that there is nothing antilyric about this deliberative structure.

Many styles of poetry bring us face to face with acts of deliberation. The eclogue is a dialogue poem about the act of choosing, as in Virgil's Third and Seventh Eclogues when a judge is asked to choose between the arguments of two shepherds. The word "eclogue" is derived from *eklegein*, meaning "to choose."[10] Another example is the tenzone, in which two poets argue "in alternating couplets," as Urban Holmes describes in *Princeton Encyclopedia of Poetry and Poetics*.[11] The tenzone eventually took on other forms, such as the partimen or jeuparti, in which one "poet proposes two hypothetical situations." One of the positions is then defended by that poet and the other by a second poet, each speaking in three stanzas.[12] In his translation of Dante's *Vita Nuova*, Mark Musa explains, "The Italian troubadours invented the sonnet form [of the tenzone], still a mode of debate in which the problem is set forth in a *proposta* inviting a *risposta* (using the same rhymes) from another poet."[13]

While in the *tenzone* two distinct sonnets are placed in dispute, an oppositional mental act is also *interior* to the sonnet itself, particularly in the Petrarchan form with its division into an octave and a sestet. While the volta, or "turn of thought," is most emphatic in the Petrarchan form, it is also recognizable in Spenserian and Shakespearean sonnets.[14]

Holmes directs attention not only to the poetic forms just enumerated but to others that entail a contest structure, such as the lauda, which calls for "responsive participation" and hence for dialogue, as well as the pastourelle, in which an aristocrat or knight attempts to seduce a shepherdess and is often outwitted by her or by her fellow shepherd.[15]

The inseparability of poetic and disputational thinking is registered in the titles of many Middle English poems: "Parlement of Foules," "Parliament of Devils," "Parliament of the Three Ages," "Dialogue between Poet and Bird," "The Cuckow and the Nightingale," "The Thrush and the Nightingale," "The Owl and the Nightingale," "The Clerk and the Nightingale," "The Floure and the Leafe," "Dispute between the Violet and the Rose," "The Holly and the Ivy," "The Debate of the Carpenter's Tools," "Wynnere and Wastoure," "Ressoning betuix Aige and Yowth," "Ressoning Betuix Deth and Man," "Death and Liffe," and, last but not least, "A Disputacion betwyx the Body and Wormes."

Medieval debate poems occur in many languages, starting with the eighth-century Carolingian poem "Conflictus Veris et Hiemis." John Edwin Wells, an early twentieth-century scholar of Middle English, notes that versions of the "Debate between Body and Soul," which first occurs in English between 1150 and 1175, "are extant in Latin, Greek, French, Provençal, German, Dutch, Spanish, Italian, Danish, and English."[16]

There are also parallels in the Eastern tradition. Titles in Sumerian, Akkadien, Assyrian, and Babylonian poems often resemble those above: "Summer contra Winter," "Bird contra Fish," "Tree contra Reed," "Silver contra Leather,"[17] "Copper vs. Leather," "Ewe vs. Wheat," "Herdsman vs. Farmer," and "Hoe vs. Plough."[18] Describing ancient Near Eastern dispute poems as "tools and toys at the same time," Herman Vanstiphout argues that a serious lesson is at the center of these poems: "All coins have two sides."[19] Much later English counterparts share this lesson. Thomas L. Reed shows that although many Anglo-Saxon and Middle English poems feature a "right" position to which the wrong thinker can be converted, in many others the disputants are equals, and no final decision is made.[20]

Reed demonstrates that in addition to all of the explicitly titled dispute poems, many of the major English works are debates: *Beowulf* with its "sparrings" and formal flytings;[21] *Piers Plowman* with its wayward and "enigmatic" path; *Sir Gawain and the Green Knight* with its disputations between green and gold, winter and summer, Christianity and chivalry, youth and age, sinner and mercy, discourtesy and treachery.[22] *The Canterbury Tales* also features a "debate on marriage" extending across the tales of the Merchant, the Clerk, the Wife of Bath, and the Franklin; the "flytings" between the Reeve, Miller, Summoner, and Friar; and the overall "narrative competition" among the taletellers to be judged by Harry Bailly.[23]

In their own time, these poems helped to give rise to new civic institutions in which disputation was carried out obsessively. Thomas Reed and Howard Bloch show the intimate connection between the "unprecedented burgeoning" of poetic disputation in the twelfth through fifteenth centuries and the simultaneous growth of three institutions: the universities, where disputation, in the forms of logic and dialectic, dominated the liberal arts;[24] the courts of law and the accompanying law school–like inns of court, where law cases and legal questions were debated in sessions called "doubts and questions," "mootings," and "boltings";[25] and the parliament, with its assembly structure and roll call votes.[26]

Just as, then, Pinker and Hunt see the sudden rise of literacy, publishing, and the novel as instigating (or at least assisting) the legal reforms that together form the Humanitarian Revolution in the eighteenth century, so the dispute structure of poetry from Homer forward helped to nourish three arenas of disputation in the twelfth and thirteenth centuries whose purpose—at least in the parliaments and law courts—is diminution of injury.[27]

What does a dispute among the muses, or between Achilles and Agamemnon, or between Sophocles and Euripides, or between two shepherds, or between a plough and a hoe, or between a rose and a violet, or between an owl and a nightingale have to do with the empathy we experience in reading *Clarissa* or *Moll Flanders* or *Emma*? In fact, the claims made about dispute greatly resemble what we can say about empathy. What they have in common is not just the recognition that there are multiple points of view, two sides to every coin, but also the chance to practice, and thereby to deepen and strengthen that recognition.

More important, both dispute and empathetic narrative require one to think counterfactually, to think the notion that one does not oneself hold to be the case. In a dispute, one side's argument may strike us as true, factual; the other side's strikes us as untrue, hence counterfactual; but we

attend to both. If we imagine a dispute poem becoming a novel, all that
has happened is that the factual side has fallen away and we are presented
only with the counterfactual. Another way to say this is that in a dispute
poem, the side one already believes in (let us say, the side of the rose) can
be understood as just a narrative excuse for introducing the side one does
not believe in (the side of the violet). By the time of fiction, the need to
lure one into the violet's story by providing the reassuring presence of the
rose has dropped out. We are just given the counterfactual from start to
finish.

The third attribute of literature that contributes to the diminution of
injury is its beauty. In this case, the reader herself may be the beneficiary;
it is the reader's own injuries that are diminished because—at least according to Walter Pater—reading extends her life. Pater observes that we
cannot actually change how long we live, but we can *effectively* do so by
"getting as many pulsations as possible into the given time." Beautiful
artworks and poems are, according to Pater, the surest way to bring about
"this quickened, multiplied consciousness" and hence to fold 200 (or perhaps 2,000) years of perception into an ordinary lifespan, which in Pater's
case was 55 years.[28]

But though the ethics of reading can surely include the benefits to the
reader herself, our focus here is on the way other, often unknown, persons
are the beneficiaries of one's reading. There are at least three paths by
which beauty contributes to this outcome.[29]

First, beautiful things (whether poems, mathematical equations, or
faces) have attributes—such as symmetry, vivacity, unity—that anticipate
those same but much more difficult to achieve attributes in the realm of
justice. Symmetry is at hand in, for example, the meter of a poem, and
provides inspiration and guidance for the centuries it will take to bring
about symmetry in the realm of justice—whether it is John Rawls's justice
as fairness, which requires "the symmetry of everyone's relations to each
another," or Plato's aspiration for a symmetry between crimes and pun-
ishments, which we are still a very long way from, or Hume's symmetry
between expectations and their fulfillment.

Second, beauty interrupts and gives us sudden relief from our own
minds. Iris Murdoch says we undergo "an unselfing" in the presence of
a beautiful thing; "self-preoccupation" and worries on one's own behalf
abruptly fall away. Simone Weil refers to this phenomenon as a "radical
decentering." I call it an "opiated adjacency," an awkward term but one
that reminds us that there are many things in life that make us feel acute
pleasure (opiated), and many things in life that make us feel sidelined, but

there is almost nothing—except beauty—that does the two simultaneously. Feeling acute pleasure at finding oneself on the margins is a first step in working toward fairness.[30]

Contact with the beautiful has one additional effect. Diotima tells Socrates who tells Plato who tells us that coming into the presence of a beautiful person or thing gives rise to the desire to bring children into the world. Diotima says contact with the beautiful also gives rise to the desire to create poems, legal treatises, and works of philosophy. Modern philosophers such as Wittgenstein have said the same. Recognizing our own capacity for creating is again a prerequisite for working for justice: While beauty can be either natural or artifactual, justice is always artifactual; it always takes immense labor to bring it about. So anything that awakens us to our own power of creation is a first step in working to eliminate asymmetries and injuries.

Literature may be able to diminish real-world injury, and the three attributes of literature—empathy, dispute, beauty—can perhaps be credited with that outcome.

Let us imagine we can do away with hesitation and affirm the open-and-shut truth of these propositions. The next question would be whether literature does its beneficial work on its own, across a diffuse, population-wide terrain, or whether its beneficent effects are accelerated by intensely individualized, person-by-person instruction. In other words, need one actively cultivate literature's curative powers?

From everything that has been said so far, it seems clear that shifts in ethical behavior require a sea change across wide populations of readers. This means, as we have long known, that the main work of the humanities is to ensure that books are placed in the hands of each incoming wave of students and carried back out to sea. Probably, though, teachers and readers need to do more. We should give more attention to making clear the lines of responsibility to real-world injuries and the call to that work that is embedded in the three key features of literature. For even if changes in sensibility will occur without instruction or explicit intervention, less mystification and more clarity might make it easier for people to find their way.

Finally, while changes in sensibility work by being widely distributed and widely shared, it would no doubt be useful to remind new readers about the changes solitary readers have made. It is clear that uniquely avid individual readers have, from time to time, made magnificent solo contributions to the diminution of injury. Daniel Defoe, the originator of the English novel, also helped originate the idea that constitutions must be written, as the legal scholar Bernadette Meyler has argued persuasively.[31]

The novel *Julie*—one of the best-selling novels with which we began—
was written by Rousseau, the author of the *Social Contract*. Hobbes, whose
Leviathan has as its central goal "getting us out of the miserable condition
of warre," read the *Iliad* often enough and rigorously enough to translate
all 16,000 lines, as he also read the *Odyssey* enough to translate that poem.
And if, with the help of J. R. Madicott's *The Origins of the English Parliament 924–1327*, we look not at the flourishing of Parliament in the twelfth
through fourteenth centuries, but at the origination of that institution,
we arrive at Æthelstan, the first king of England, in the early tenth century. He turned what in earlier reigns had been an ad hoc procedure of
occasionally consulting advisors into a formal, regular assembly that wit-
nessed and approved charters and laws.[32] Æthelstan was known for his
book collecting, his learning, and for the poems that emerged from his
court (including, it seems probable, *De arte metrica*, a treatise on poetry
written in verse). There is evidence, though far from conclusive, that *Beowulf* was written in his circle.[33] "The quantity of poetry to survive from
this reign," biographer Sarah Foot writes, "suggests that poetry recitation
may have formed a part of evening entertainment at his court."[34]

No matter how loyal and unswerving one's personal and public
commitments—to a love partner, a country, an idea—part of our interior
remains capable of change. It is this part of our interior—this region of
reversibility that is like a sheet of spun fabric one nanometer thick—that
literature addresses. Far from being a threat to our commitments, this interior silk fabric that makes us labile and open enables us actively to re-consent
each day to the people and places we are ever more deeply committed to. It
also makes us open to new commitments. All genres of literature address
this part of us: That is why anti-theatrical tracts are so frightened of the
theatre; that is why it is impossible to predict which fictional person any
one of us will identify with when reading *Antony and Cleopatra* or *Wuthering
Heights*.

But it is not just that literature addresses this counterfactual fabric, this
honeycombed pliancy within one's thoughts and spirit. It is that literature—
centuries of literature—has created it, or at least enabled it to remain intact
even after we are old enough to have become "completed" persons.[35]

The Ethics of Reading

Charles Larmore

What can be meant by "the ethics of reading" is not immediately obvious. The phrase has become popular in contemporary literary criticism largely through the influence of J. Hillis Miller.[1] What it suggests is that reading is a practice that raises questions of ethical significance. Yet why this should be so can seem puzzling and the writings of literary critics who invoke the phrase have done little to dispel the obscurity. Consider the term "ethics" itself. In the philosophical tradition, ethics as a discipline has been concerned with two distinct though interrelated questions: how we ought to live in order to live well, and how we are to treat one another and perhaps other living beings as well. In recent times, the term has also been used to refer, more specifically, to the first of these subjects in contrast to the second, which is then commonly classified as "morality." Now in what way does reading constitute an ethical phenomenon in either of these two respects? Certainly, we live richer lives if we read some good books, and there are likewise many cases in which reading various materials (ranging from newspapers to the Bible, say), and reading them well, can deepen our understanding of how we ought to act with regard to others. But talk about an "ethics of reading" has, I believe, something more essential in mind, namely, that our very relation as readers to what we read—to books or more generally to texts—is of ethical significance. How can this be so? This is the question I will pursue, though my answer will be rather different from the sort that many literary critics would be inclined to accept.

The most basic fact about our relation as readers to texts is that this relation is asymmetrical. We can read the text, but the text cannot read us. Sometimes, I know, literary critics talk about "being read by the text," but this is a metaphorical usage, referring to the experience of being challenged by the text to reflect on some of our central assumptions, an experience we can have only in and through our reading of the text. Reading is an act, initiated and performed by an agent, and texts themselves are not agents: Texts speak to us only when they are read, and read by us. Now if the reading relation is essentially asymmetrical, and if it is moreover a relation not to another person, but to something else, namely, to a text, how can it be a relation that is, in itself, of an ethical character?

You may feel that I have left out another equally essential feature of our relation as readers to what we read: Though the text that we read is not another person, it was written by a person to embody his or her thinking and feeling. I think this point is right and, moreover, absolutely crucial. If a text is not conceived as being the expression of its author's intention, then the practice of reading cannot itself be of intrinsic ethical significance. We may consider the ways that reading enriches the lives of readers or gives them instruction about how to treat others well, and in this sense we can talk about the ethical importance of reading, that is, about its beneficial consequences. But there can be an "ethics of reading" that regards the practice of reading as itself a matter of ethical moment only if the relation of reader to text is ultimately a relation of the reader to another person. However, I want to postpone a clarification of the problematic notion of "author's intention" (I shall return to it shortly) in order to focus on the salient fact about the reading relation, which is that it connects us to another person only indirectly. In the act of reading, the author is not there, only the text. For it is this fact—the author's absence—that constitutes what is special in the ethical character of the practice of reading.

That reading in this regard, given the absence of the author, gives rise to a special sort of ethical problem is glimpsed by Plato in his discussion of writing at the end of his dialogue, the *Phaedrus*. I say "glimpsed" because Plato's main concern in that passage lies with the dangers of writing rather than with the responsibilities of reading, although the two are connected and although one of the remarks that Plato has Socrates make points to what must be the fundamental concern of an "ethics of reading." The trouble with a text, Socrates says, is that "roaming about everywhere" it comes to be read both by those who are intelligent readers and by those who are not, and yet it is by nature unable to defend itself against the abuses of misunderstanding that may be perpetrated by the latter: "When it is wronged (*plemmeloumenos*) and attacked unfairly (*ouk en dikei*), it always stands in need of its father's support, for on its own it can neither defend itself nor come to its own support." (275e). By "its father" is meant, of course, the author of the text, and Plato is claiming that the text itself, unlike its author, cannot correct the misinterpretations by which readers may treat it unfairly as they fail to listen to what it says or distort its meaning for their own purposes.

Now it is essential to distinguish the two parts of Plato's claim: that (1) the text cannot talk back and object to an interpretation of its meaning that has been foisted upon it, and that (2) the author, if he or she were present, could authoritatively correct the erroneous interpretation. We need not accept the second part—in fact, we ought not to accept it since it is untrue (I will have more to say about this)—in order to recognize the crucial importance of the first part for the idea of an "ethics of reading." It is a corollary of the essential asymmetry of the reading relation that I underscored before. When people are wronged, they are in principle (if they have not been killed in the process) able to object to their mistreatment. Texts, by contrast, cannot object to how they are mistreated—that is, to how they are inadvertently, carelessly, or deliberately misread. In this fact lies, as I have suggested, the special ethical significance of the reading relation.

However, the practice of reading can have an ethical character at all and there can be such a thing as an ethics of reading only if, as I have also argued, our relation as readers to texts is ultimately, if not directly, a relation to another person. The text must be understood to be the expression of its author's intention. Moreover, if misreading the text consists in failing to grasp what the text itself says—and what else could misreading mean, if it is to mean anything at all?—then what the text says, and in this sense its meaning, must be defined by the author's intention. Since I have rejected the idea that the author is the authoritative interpreter of a text's meaning, I need to say how I think the notion of author's intention should be conceived.[2]

That this notion is indispensable, on at least some construal, ought to be indisputable; unfortunately, among literary and hermeneutic theorists it is not. Texts do not write themselves. They are written by authors and are written to some purpose or variety of purposes. If we did not suppose that the text was the expression of the author's intention, we would have no basis for thinking, as we do, that to understand the meaning of some problematic passage we should turn, first of all if not exclusively, to other passages of the same text or to other writings by the same author. We consider them to be directly pertinent because we presume that they have been produced by the same cause as the passage in question, namely, the mind of the given author.

Yet the term "the author's intention" can signify a number of different things. In some of its senses—what the author set out to say, what he said to himself as he composed the text, what he may have said afterward about his aims—the author's intention need not coincide with the text's meaning. Contrary to Plato, the author (though usually a commentator of interest) is not the authoritative interpreter of what a text says. That is because what the text means consists in what it itself says, and not in what the author says about it. Yet the author's intention in still a further sense—namely, what the author intended insofar as he realized this intention in the composition of the text, with whatever degree of self-awareness—must count as determining what the text itself says or means. For again, if it is possible to misunderstand a text, then there must be something that the text actually says, and as texts do not write themselves, what they say can only be what their authors meant in the very process of writing them as they did.

To be sure, we do not read books solely for their textual meaning. We do not aim only, or even principally, to determine what a book's author meant to say, but rather seek to discover what the book means for us. We may, for instance, be interested in seeing how it forms part of a larger cultural movement or in charting its influence on other works. More commonly, we may want to find out how it speaks to our own interests and preoccupations. If it is a legal text (a statute, judicial opinion, or constitutional provision), we may want to ascertain its import for a particular case or social problem. However, all these endeavors require that we first form an idea of what the text itself says or means. For how else can we gauge its relevance in these various ways? And what it means, as I have argued, consists in the author's intention as realized in the text itself. The distinction between a text's *meaning* in this sense and its *significance*, its relevance to the reader's concerns, is indispensable (though I think there are often errors in the way this distinction is drawn, for instance, by E. D. Hirsch).[3] True, part of the author's intention is normally that the work be in some way significant for its readers; yet intended and actual significance are obviously two quite different things. I know that many literary theorists dismiss the notion of authorial intention and even the notion of textual meaning. But without these concepts, we can make no sense of such basic features of the reading process as the possibility of misreading and the perception of relevance.

Having clarified the idea of author's intention, I return to the ethics of reading. My thesis has been that there can be an ethics of reading only if the reading relation is itself ethical in nature. It is so, I have argued, in that it is ultimately a relation to another person, namely, the author. However, I have also been arguing that the ethical nature of the reading relation is special in character because it relates us to that person only in the form of a text, which, unlike a person, is unable to object to how it may be mistreated—that is, to how it may be misread. Indeed, even if the author were there as we read and objected that we were misinterpreting what he had written, his interpretation of the text's meaning would not be necessarily correct, nor ours necessarily wrong. No one can speak authoritatively for the text, and the text cannot defend itself.

Now because of this difference between the text and its author—the text is not itself a person, nor what it says or means the property of its author—one might ask whether the reading relation is in fact an ethical relation and whether there can therefore be such a thing as the ethics of reading. Is misreading a text really to wrong the author? I think it is, particularly when the misreading is not simply inadvertent, but the result of carelessness or deliberate distortion. Consider the case of actions, which are not so unlike texts. Suppose that someone regards the actions of a certain person as of so little consequence that he fails to see the other's gesture for the generous offer it is or finds it useful for his own interests to portray that offer as something altogether different, say, as an attempt at ingratiation. Surely we would think that he has wronged the other person, even though the immediate object of the wrong was the other's action (which has been thoughtlessly or perfidiously construed) and even though that action is neither itself a person (and so cannot defend itself) nor the property of the agent, whose statements after the fact about his intentions are not authoritative. The agent has been wronged because what he was doing in acting as he did has been slighted or deliberately falsified. It is similar, I believe, with authors and texts.

Texts do differ from actions in an important respect. Agents are generally in the vicinity of their actions, so when their actions are described falsely, or when they believe that they are, they can object. Texts, by contrast, "roam about everywhere" (*kulindeitai pantachou*), as Plato says, and do not have their authors nearby, or necessarily anyone, to stand up for them when they are misread. To write a text, to express something of oneself in writing, is thus to make oneself especially vulnerable to others. In this fact there appears the ultimate import of the ethics of reading: it highlights the very essence of the ethical outlook. In general, the moral point of view consists in seeing in another's good a reason for action on our part, apart from all consideration of our own good. As a result, our ethical character shows itself most clearly in how we treat the vulnerable, since they cannot make it in our interest to treat them well. Though I will not go so far as to say that a bad reader cannot be a good person, I doubt that a habitually careless or deliberately manipulative reader will be one.

I close with a similar observation by Karl Kraus, the Viennese satirist and moralist, about the respect for language in all its forms. It is, he said, a "mental discipline that enjoins the highest measure of responsibility toward the sole thing that can be wronged with impunity, namely language, and that serves like no other to teach respect for every other kind of human good."[4]

Responses and Discussion

Kwame Anthony Appiah

The essays by Elaine Scarry and Charles Larmore are very stimulating, suggesting, as they do, two ways to construe the idea of an ethics of reading. Let me say something about each of them in turn, and then I will sketch the beginnings of an account of my own.

Larmore began, I thought, with the right problem: We know we can be responsible to people, and we have some idea of what that entails. But to speak of a responsibility to a text seems like anthropomorphism. Philosophers are fine with anthropomorphism, but here, as with all figures, we would like to find a literal truth they point to. To find something to which we can be more literally responsible, he suggests that we have to start with the thought that "though the text . . . is not another person, it was written by a person to embody his or her thinking and feeling." He goes on to propose that our responsibility as readers just is our responsibility to the author.

I am not sure I agree. And I would like to sketch, in an admittedly rather abstract and perfunctory way, the basis of my disagreements, as I think there are important issues at stake.

Larmore says, "if it is possible to misunderstand a text, then there must be something that the text actually says, and since texts do not write themselves, what they say can only be what their authors meant in the very process of writing them as they did."

I think there are two problems here. First, it seems to me that literary reading only begins with what the text says, and so it is not best explained as seeking to know what it says. Second, the thing that starts the process of literary reading—which is indeed, I grant, what the text says—is a property of the words it uses that runs free of the author's ambitions for them. The task of figuring out what someone wrote is not the task of figuring out her intentions but the task of figuring out the intentions with which the inscription she wrote is associated by linguistic conventions. These two will coincide in only the most barebones cases of literal nonfiction.

In any case, while literary reading begins with what the text says and what the text says has little to do with the actual intentions of its author, what is literarily *interesting* about the text is almost never what it says but many of the other things it does, only some of which it does with what it says. To understand these other effects, we need both to understand conventions beyond the linguistic—narrative conventions, prosodic rules, and the like—and to find things to say about those effects. Inspired by reading a single limerick of Edward Lear's, one might write a poem that almost shared its form. It might go like this:

There was a young bard from Japan
Whose limericks never would scan.
When asked why this was,
He said, "It's because
I always try to get as many words into the last line as I possibly can."

In explaining what is going on here, we need to refer to the metrical conventions of the limerick; they do their work because this poem breaches them, whether or not it was the author's intention to do so. Now, of course, in this case it would be an extremely strange hypothesis that the actual poet did not know about these conventions, as the poem's joke depends on them. But my point is that we need no independent access to the poet's intentions here, so it does not matter what they actually were.

Indeed, as far as I know, this limerick, like many other famous limericks, is anonymous. We know almost nothing about the author. It would seem strange to be concerned with the aims of a person about whom we know (and care) so little in beginning to approach this verse. This also counts against this approach.

Larmore suggests that our responsibility to the text is a responsibility to the author and that sloppy reading misrepresents, and thus wounds, the author. Perhaps that is so, though these are wounds that do not cause much actual suffering. But a sloppy reading that is not attentive to the conventions, linguistic and literary, that constrain a reading betrays not just the author but all those whose conventions they are. Whether this is a betrayal that rises to the level of a moral harm—whether, that is, it is something we should not do because of what we owe to others—I am less certain.

But it is a kind of wrong: it is a betrayal of a notion of reading. And that notion is *our* notion, the conception of us as a community of critics and scholars and readers. In perpetrating it, it seems to me, you betray us. The literary life of our cultures is a collectively created good, produced by the participants' conformity to (and, as the limerick reminds us, occasional defection from) its conventions. The defections need to have a detectable purpose—a purpose visible in them, so to speak—if they are to be contributions. (One way of making a defection detectable would be to announce it, of course.) Without the contributions of conventional responses and motivated defections, we would not have a literary culture.

I am almost totally in sympathy with Scarry's essay. I agree in finding it plausible that the forms of reading literature that criticism aims to enable sometimes diminish injury. I am inclined to think, too, that the incitement to empathy and to disciplined deliberation are central to that moral achievement. And I agree with her when she connects these two things. What they have in common is not just the recognition but also the chance to practice (and thereby deepen and strengthen) the recognition, that there are multiple points of view, two sides to every coin.

I should say that the fact that I agree with these claims is the result of reading her essay, and is not something I had grasped before; so I am grateful to her for her essay and its arguments. She claims a role for beauty in literature's ethical achievement as well; only this thought was not new to me, as I had learned it from her earlier.

If I were to offer my own positive account of an ethics of reading, it would start like this: Reading has norms, which develop alongside but independently of the texts we read. They are not mostly ethical norms; that is, they are not simply applications of the broader ethical norms that fix how we ought to treat one another and what it is for a human life to go well. But, as Scarry shows, there are ways in which profound ethical issues in this sense are addressed and ethical projects are advanced by literature and its readings.

As readers, our conformity to literary conventions, like the conformity to norms of prosody or plot for writers, is what is needed for reading to work as a practice. We can do other things with texts than read them, in this sense; but to offer a reading of a text to others is to commit to the developing practice. The points of the practice are not external to it, and, as I say, they develop. But like all artistic practices, reading flourishes only when people—as creators and as audience—are committed to continuing an ongoing conversation. That is the commitment that I think gives reading an ethics in the first place: It generates obligations to others, as does our participation in any human project from which we benefit. That is why misreading can amount, as I said, to betrayal.

Jonathan Culler

Is there an ethics of reading? There seem to be several. For Wayne Booth, who brought the topic of the ethics of reading to the fore, it is a question of the ethics guiding the reader's decisions about what to read: "Which of the world's narratives," he asked "should now be banned or embraced in the lifetime project of building the character of an ethical reader?"[1] What models should a reader embrace, and specifically how does a reader negotiate between a tradition of exclusion/purification (in which you behave ethically by rejecting the impure), and one of embracing everything human, if only to test every supposed virtue? The question for Booth was what choices to make for the best ethical training.

This is related to one aspect of Elaine Scarry's wide-ranging paper, specifically to her claim about the ethical effects of reading literature for encouraging empathy and justice, but it is not the same question. It would be nice if Scarry's argument about the ethical effects of reading were true; perhaps it is true, but I am reminded of Françoise in Proust's *A la recherche du temps perdu*, who, when the pregnant kitchen maid was suffering the most appalling pains, was sent to fetch a book about them and much later was found weeping copiously at the description of the symptoms, crying, "O holy virgin, is it possible that God wishes any wretched human creature to suffer so?" But when she came back into the kitchen maid's presence, Proust writes, "at the sight of those very sufferings, the printed account of which had moved her to tears, she had nothing to offer but ill-tempered mutterings, mingled with bitter sarcasm."[2]

I want to focus instead on what I take to be the more recent question about the ethics of reading—put forward by J. Hillis Miller and Derek Attridge, as addressed by Charles Larmore: To what extent does our own reading involve an ethical relation to the text? Larmore claims that if there is an ethical relation to the text, this must be based on a relation to the author as person, but I am not convinced.

One possible reading activity involves commitment to revealing the truth of the text. In *Getting It Right: Language, Literature, and Ethics*, a book that has not been as widely read as it should be, Geoffrey Harpham (who could not be present at this symposium because of an ethical choice—his daughter is getting married) writes not about the ethics of reading but about what he calls "The Ethics of Analysis." This is a high-powered account of a process of strong reading in a variety of fields and contexts. Here, the ethics of reading is not at all a quest for the diminution of pain. Rather, it is a matter of paradoxical necessity for effective analysis of the truth of the text. "The task of the analyst," Harpham writes, with some ironic distance, "is to overcome the resistance of a coded, indirect, metaphorical, fragmentary or occluded utterance, and to produce a version that is represented as being in certain respects truer than the original, while remaining true to the original." That is, the analyst claims to reveal what is really going on in this text. But, Harpham continues,

> If the first requirement of the secondary text is that it represent the primary text, then the analyst must undergo an act of repression in which his self-sufficiency, his autonomy are humbled and subjected to the imperative of the text, a submission to what the primary text actually says, and therefore compels him to say.[3]

This is a complex process in which, as one exposes what the previous text truly says, one performs an act of violence, drives it into a position of dependence on one's own text that will reveal the truth of the original; but at the same time, in this structure one is subjecting oneself to the structures and demands of the text being read, setting aside one's own desires and prejudices in order to read the text truly. This process involves not respect for the author (since one claims to show that the author did not truly grasp the truth of his or her own text), but a peculiar ethics of reading that follows from the commitment to reveal the truth of a text. But this is only one of many modes of reading.

There are situations in which it seems right to expect a reader to behave ethically toward an author—the best case scenario for Larmore's model. For instance, when writing a review of a book, a professional expectation is that you will read the whole book, attempt to understand the project from the author's point of view, and describe the argument or vision before criticizing it, and when criticizing it not distort or misrepresent. Ethical considerations arise here, it seems to me, not because of anything about the nature of reading but because (1) you are writing about the book for a public and (2) you are doing so in a context where you are expected to inform. If you choose to write polemically about a book that has been published for some time and has already been reviewed, especially in a case where there is controversy, there is no need to try to grasp the author's perspective or treat the author ethically. Your ethical obligation, rather, is to your own readers: that you not deceive *them* as you make your arguments about the errors of the author's ways. It seems to me *a fortiori* the case that one has no ethical obligation to the author of a text when the author is dead. Attempting to do justice to Marx or Freud, to treat them properly, not as a means to an end but as an end in itself, is perfectly acceptable, but this is only one possible project; it is equally valid simply to *use* the texts of Marx or Freud as resources for argument or foils to define your own views more distinctly. Again I would say that the ethical obligation is to your own readers, not to a dead author.

 When you are *not* writing or speaking publicly about a book but only reading it, I cannot see that the question of an ethics of reading arises. This is not because I deny that texts are the expression of their authors' intentions. To claim that one has an ethical obligation to the work because it is the expression of the views of a person seems to me to cheapen the notion of an ethical relation to persons by diluting it. To say that I owe the same obligations to all the books in the library as I do to my neighbor is to deny that there is anything at all special about my obligation to treat another person ethically. It may be wrong to ignore someone who is speaking to you, and it may be somewhat unethical completely to ignore what someone is trying to tell you; but there is nothing wrong with skipping pages or whole chapters of a book to see if there is anything there that interests you. It may be wrong to attribute motives or presuppositions to a friend without giving him or her an opportunity to respond, but attributing motives or presuppositions to a text that we are reading is an important mode of analysis.

It is perhaps true that in the case of a novel the ideal relation of a reader to the text is one that simulates an ethical relation to persons, that tries fully to enter the imaginative world of the work, to give the author every benefit of the doubt and so on, but this is only one of many possible modes of reading. Most of the reading we do is very different; we look for things relevant to our concerns, for ideas or information that will stimulate us. We pace our reading not according to notions of what is required for justice to an author but according to our own interests. We read carefully when it seems important, and skim or skip altogether when it does not. There is nothing wrong with that. Authors put their texts into the world for un-known readers to use as they will—that is one of the gambles of authorship. Your text may encounter people who will despise your work and you, who dismiss it out of hand, as well as those who read carefully or self-effacingly. Authors cannot expect care and diligence from every reader.

So I do want to challenge the notion of an ethics of reading, which seems to me to have been designed by literary critics to make their activity look more ethical, at a time when much literary criticism was accused of being nihilistic or worse. I understand the notion of the singularity of the work of art, which makes it a little bit like a person, but one of the exciting differences is that we can do with the work what we will, without harm. We have to respect persons; we cannot creatively mold them into something else. But with works we can. We can quote selectively; we can parody or transform. Even if one does not accept Harold Bloom's notion of the history of literature as a history of strong misreading, a history of belated authors trying to slay the strong precursor in oedipal battles, it is certainly the case that piety toward the predecessor text has seldom ac-complished much. Jean-Francois Lyotard in *Le différend* goes so far as to depict the reader as "the persecutor of the work," who holds it hostage, to make it show what it means.[4]

So I would deny that ethical treatment of the work is the ideal. Wayne Booth, who inaugurated this line of thinking before it was taken up by J. Hillis Miller and Derek Attridge, introduced a distinction that I think is important, between *understanding* and *overstanding*. Understanding in-volves what we might generally think of as ethical reading: trying to un-derstand a work on its own terms, in the ways in which an author might have conceived and intended it. Understanding is asking the questions and finding the answers that the text insists on. "Once upon a time there were three little pigs . . ." demands that we ask, "So what happened?" not "Why three?" or "What is the concrete historical context?" (both exam-ples of overstanding). Booth prefers understanding to overstanding, but he recognizes that it can be very productive to ask questions that the au-thor does not intend us to ask. To illustrate overstanding he writes,

What do you have to say, you seemingly innocent child's tale of three little pigs and a wicked wolf, about the culture that preserves and responds to you? About the unconscious dreams of the author or folk that created you? About the history of narrative suspense? About the relations of the lighter and the darker races? About big people and little people, hairy and bald, lean and fat? About triadic patterns in human history? About the Trinity? About laziness and industry, family structure, domestic architecture, dietary practice, standards of justice and revenge? About the history of manipulations of narrative point of view for the creation of sympathy? Is it good for a child to read you or hear you recited, night after night? Will stories like you—*should* stories like you—be allowed when we have produced our ideal socialist state? What are the sexual implications of that chimney—or of this strictly male world in which sex is never mentioned? What about all that huffing and puffing?[5]

Good questions all, though they might be said to manhandle the text. If ethical reading involves attempting to grasp the author's realized intention, these are questions that do not lead that way. Asking what the text conceals or represses is not reading according to our model for ethical dealings with a person, but it is important for critical reflection.

I'd like to conclude by quoting G. K. Chesterton, who wrote, "Either literary criticism is no good at all (a thoroughly defensible proposition) or else criticism consists of saying about an author those very things that would have made him jump out of his boots."[6]

Derek Attridge

In reading Charles Larmore's essay, I very consciously made an effort to understand exactly what he meant to say. This I could only do, of course, by attending closely to the sense of the words and their syntactic organization, with due regard to the generic conventions of the academic paper. But I read always with the assumption that the text was the embodiment of a clear intention. I was on the alert for tonal subtleties, especially irony of any sort, which would have demanded some adjustment to the literal meaning of the sentences (though in fact irony seemed to be absent). My careful attention was partly due, it is true, to my knowledge that I would eventually have to account for my reading before a sophisticated and astute audience, but an important impetus to scrupulousness was also what I would regard as my responsibility as the reader of a philosophical text.

That responsibility is ultimately to the *author* of the text, a responsibility awakened by the fact of the author's mental labor in producing a verbal artifact; to read sloppily or with a closed mind would be to slight that labor and to do an injustice to the author. This, then, would be an example of the ethics of reading. ·

It is an example that accords wholly with Larmore's argument, with which I have no quarrel in its application to a text such as his own. My difficulties begin when I try to apply the argument to a literary text (or, as I would prefer to say, a literary *work*, for reasons that I will come to in a little while). Early in his discussion, Larmore asserts, as an "absolutely crucial" point: "Though the text that we read is not another person, it was written by a person *to embody his or her thinking*" (emphasis mine). Though this description might be appropriate for literary scientists like Lucretius or Erasmus Darwin, it seems wholly inadequate for the creative process of most poets, novelists, or playwrights. But let us assume that what Larmore *really* meant when he wrote this sentence (and I realize that in distinguishing between what the words say and what the author "*really* meant" I am already casting a bit of a shadow over my initial agreement) was that it was written by a person to embody his or her thinking, feeling, imagining, intuiting, hoping, and all the many other experiences that may go into the creation of a literary work. With this rereading, it becomes possible to agree with Larmore that even in the case of literature "the practice of reading can have an ethical character at all and there can be such a thing as an ethics of reading only if . . . our relation as readers to texts is ultimately, if not directly, a relation to another person."

Or, I should say, it becomes possible to agree if we make another modification: "another person" should surely be "another person or persons." If I read a medieval mystery play, I am aware that the words have been shaped by many hands, probably across many generations; if I read Robert Lowell's English version of Racine's *Phèdre*, I am enjoying both the crafting of the French play by the latter and the power of the English verse composed by the former. (If I witness a *performance* of one of these plays, of course, I also have to take into account the creativity of the actors, the designer, the director, and perhaps others as well as the various authorial originators, a point to which I will return.) "Intention" is starting to look like a less and less useful word when it is literature we are dealing with— something that should not surprise us after all the ink that has been spilled over it in the debates of literary theory.

In any case, intention as Larmore describes it does not sound very much like intention in the ordinary sense of the word—and in my responsible reading of his text, it is my obligation to try to ascertain exactly how he is using it. What we might assume to be the intention "behind" the text, perhaps checkable against the author's own statements about his or her intention, appears to be something quite different: Intention in his paper is referred to not as something behind the text, but as co-extensive with it. Thus "misreading" is defined as "failing to grasp what the text itself says" (we might note that for a moment the text has become an agent); we are told that "what the text says depends on the text itself"; and the notion of intention is importantly qualified by the assertion that the author's intention must count "insofar as he realized this intention in the composition of the text." This is puzzling, as it had seemed that Larmore was talking about texts in general (and perhaps not literary texts at all), yet the identification of the author's intention with "the text itself" rather than what the author wanted to say is not something we associate with more quotidian texts. If a journalist writes a piece that appears to defame a public figure, the former can say with perfect good sense, "I did not intend to defame so-and-so"; he or she may be lying—the piece may indeed be defamatory—but it remains the case that in an instance of this kind intention cannot be identified with "what the text says."

In the case of the literary work, however, this understanding of intention makes more sense. It means that an ethical reading of a literary work is one that attends with care and with an open mind to the meanings of the words, as captured by means of the publicly shared knowledge of the language, the appropriate generic conventions, the histories of usage, and so on. Because of the problems they raise, I would prefer to ditch the words "intention" and "text" and speak in terms of the author's *work*, a word that nicely combines the labor of creation and the created artifact. One way of representing this shift in approach is that the focus is not on what literary uses of language have in common with all uses of language—which appears to be Larmore's method—but what literary works have in common with all artworks. The viewer of a painting or the listener to a piece of music are also ethical agents whose responsibility is to the creator or creators of the work (and in the latter case, to the performer or performers as well). What these works "say"—the word is becoming a little problematic now—or what they mean is unlikely to be convertible into language, but then what a literary work means is equally resistant to linguistic conversion. Just because a literary work uses language as its medium is not a reason for thinking that its meaning is purely linguistic. If we think of the work of art as an *event* rather than a set of signs to be decoded, and the reader's response as an *experience* rather than a meaning to be carried away, we are less likely to fall into this trap. And focusing on the reader's experience makes it possible to shift from a notion of the "author"—always too easily identified with the flesh-and-blood individual—to what I have termed elsewhere "authoredness": the assumption that the words we are reading emanate from a historical creative agent, whose exact character (individual, sequence of individuals, group; known or unknown) is irrelevant but whose real existence cannot be doubted.

In discussing literature, then, I am not able to accept Larmore's assertion that what texts say "can only be what their authors meant in the very process of writing them as they did." And I am not talking about the *significance* of literary works (if the distinction between meaning and significance is a sustainable one, about which I have my doubts); I am talking about *meaning*, though this has to include the meanings generated by, for instance, the handling of plot, metaphor, rhythm, and diction. Meaning is also inseparable from *context:* When I turn to other passages by the author to clarify what I am reading, I am not searching for an intention, as Larmore suggests, but rather I am following the normal practice of using context to determine sense. An author's oeuvre, like a single work of art or the art of a particular period, constitutes just such a usable context.

Yet I want to emphasize as well my agreement with Larmore that if reading—at least the reading of literary works—is a matter of ethics, this is because the reader has a responsibility not just to the words being read (which I think is a dubious concept), but to the creator (or creators) of the work of art they constitute. If we can assume that what is at stake is the literary work, I am very much in sympathy with Larmore when he states, "To write a text, to express something of oneself in writing, is . . . to make oneself especially vulnerable to others," and when he goes on to argue that our treatment of the vulnerable is a particularly revealing test of our ethical character. There are echoes here, no doubt unintentional (in the common or garden variety sense of the word), of one of the most demanding of ethical thinkers, Emmanuel Levinas. For Levinas, ethics inheres in responsibility for the other—and he names the other "par excellence," using the Biblical phrasing, as "the widow, the orphan and the stranger." Although Levinas would have had no truck with the willingness on both Larmore's and my part to extend the notion of responsibility to include the reader's response to the inaccessible and sometimes unknown creator of the literary work, his work—as much literary as it is philosophical, perhaps—captures with great power what might be thought of as the ethics of reading.

Unlike Larmore, Elaine Scarry addresses very specifically the matter of the reading of *literature*. However, it is only her third question that relates closely to the issues that I have been discussing. The first two questions are empirical in nature, and it may simply be the case that the evidence is unavailable and inaccessible. Claims about literature's efficacy in producing large-scale improvements in ethical behavior are purely post hoc. Even if it could be shown that there is a connection, it is hard to see how particular attributes of literature could be singled out as responsible for it. Empathy, disputation, and beauty are neither peculiar nor essential to literature. Similar or perhaps stronger claims could be made for many other characteristics of literary reading that have important ethical implications, such as scrupulousness, open-mindedness, and imaginativeness.

Scarry's third question is not empirical but is itself ethical: Should the reader or teacher work actively to cultivate and instill the ethical force of literature? Here she and I are in agreement: Readers and teachers of literature *do* have an ethical responsibility, though I would characterize it not so much as "making clear the lines of responsibility to real-world injuries" or providing reminders of "the changes solitary readers have made," but rather as the obligation to do justice to the inventiveness and singularity of the literary work, and thus to the achievement of its author or authors. This capacity for responsible responsiveness demands of the reader an openness to change, a quality Scarry has rather wonderfully described by means of the metaphor of an internal silk fabric—a metaphor that, for me, is the most powerful moment of her essay.

Discussion Session 1: The Ethics of Reading

DUNCAN WRIGHT: Elaine Scarry, you gave a beautiful example of literature as an ethical project, as enlarging our sympathies. Do you also think we can say that reading helps us understand and recognize manipulation in society and in culture?

ELAINE SCARRY: First, I never think there is a one-to-one relationship between someone who reads literature and someone who acts ethically. The example given of Françoise in Proust's work has counterpart examples in the works of Pushkin, Tolstoy, and James—say, of a character crying at the opera and then not attending to a coachman freezing on the theater steps. But I do think glacially, over a large population, that one's ability to think counterfactually and pliantly does absolutely make one better at attending to misuses and manipulations of language.

RICHARD SENNETT: Do you draw a distinction between empathy and sympathy in your work? I think of sympathy as identification with someone else—Adam Smith's theory of moral sentiment and putting yourself in the place of another. Empathy is attention to someone with whom you cannot identify, and the mode is more curiosity than identification. Empathy is a more powerful force ethically. It creates a public realm in a way that sympathy does not because we are honoring the stranger, attending to someone we may not like or understand or know. I wonder if that is a useful distinction for you?

ES: It probably is a useful distinction; I have heard others make it, and I am never sensitive enough to what is at stake in the distinction. One thing that is important in the reading I am talking about is a kind of self-erasure, a putting aside of the self. I would see the ideas that Derek Attridge raised about imaginative freedom and attention as very bound up in it.

MARJORIE CURRY WOODS: As someone working in medieval and classical literature, I was grateful that you brought many of those texts into your discussion. I also work on the tradition of boys empathizing, and to some extent sympathizing, with women characters like Dido. There seems to be no direct correlation between that identification and social action. Suzanne Keen has discussed this lack of direct social action resulting from empathy or sympathy.[1] But I think if we tie this only to social action and what goes on outside the classroom, it might blind us to the fact that these exercises may help with creativity and the learning of literature. Finally, it does seem that if these kinds of sympathetic readings are happening very early historically in our literature, it has not changed our ethics very quickly.

ES: Right, it's not that I read and then I go out and care more about people. It's glacial and over time. I may be completely wrong about this causal connection but I do literally believe it is the case. We can see it not only in medieval texts but in ancient Greece, in the part the Panathenaeum plays—the recitation of poetry—in giving rise to the Lyceum, to the assembly, and to the jury. Plato quotes Homer 150 times—I think he knows the poem by heart.

On the issue of empathy, it is both celebrated and berated. Empathy tends to be celebrated more outside the discipline of literary studies, and I think both views have to be listened to. I listen very carefully to the voices outside because when you are inside a discipline you never step outside the frame in order to see the central questions. You are inside the frame of the discipline, whereas people outside keep having to step over the frame. When you talk to ordinary readers outside the discipline—and I mean serious, intelligent readers—they are often reading primarily for this act of sympathetic or empathetic identification. This practice doesn't go away (even if it is rightly critiqued sometimes) because I think it is such a fundamental attribute of reading.

ERICA KISS: This is a question for Charles Larmore. Your model about the intention expressed in the work actually, to me, describes propaganda or a propagandistic text rather than literature, in that you assume a strong agency or purpose in the work. In artistic works, you do not quite have this expression of a purpose; purposiveness in the work tends to be implied. The semantic strategy in artistic utterance is not that the author expresses a purpose that the reader is obliged to understand. The semantic strategy is more like gambling, where you imply something, thereby risking not to be understood in a specific, predetermined manner. This allows an interpretive freedom in literature that is not available in propaganda.

CHARLES LARMORE: The way I think one ought to approach the question of interpreting literary texts is by first of all understanding what it means to interpret texts of an ordinary sort. To do that, I think it is helpful to understand how to interpret human actions. When we try to interpret someone else's actions, we try to figure out what that person was intending to do. We don't necessarily assume she is fully or even partially aware of what she was trying to do. Her own reports about what she was trying to do are no doubt evidence, but we don't assume that she is an authoritative interpreter of her own action.

I understand what you mean, that in literary texts intention may not be directly expressed. A literary text does not begin with a topic sentence; it may proceed by implication. Literary texts are much more complex, elaborately structured artifacts. But I think in the first instance we are trying to find out why certain things are in the text and others not. It is a causal question, and the place to look for the cause is the author. It is not that the author is in sovereign control, and the sovereign herself may be shaped by all sorts of factors of which she is not aware, but all of this is part of what the text means. So I think we need to proceed first from an understanding of how we interpret human action. This is the historical basis for hermeneutics. Schleiermacher worked out his theory of textual interpretation by looking first at what it is to interpret a meaningful utterance in general.

BROOKE HOLMES: Back to the issue of authorial intent, I am not thinking about the ethics of reading as necessarily an obligation to an author, but more as a challenge to how we instrumentalize texts. That is, texts push back, become resistant, not because we have offended the intention of the author but because we are being forced as readers to become more pliable, to think differently or to occupy a different perspective. Our intention that we may have come with to instrumentalize a text in a certain way may be thwarted, may not be allowed in the close reading. Reading texts from another historical period in particular may have this ethical dimension.

Also, thinking about metrics, I wonder if we need to justify this ethics of reading in real-world effects. Or is there a way to articulate more robustly the value of this practice that is not dependent on external effects, a value competitive with those that might be produced by the social sciences? Or do we just end up having to say we believe in its good effects?

ES: Maybe some alternative set of values could be more explicit. We don't talk about beauty much, and I think that omission would not be so harmful except for the fact that advertisers are every day telling us that when we see something of beauty we should buy it, whereas centuries of poets and philosophers say that when you see something beautiful you should begin to repair the injuries of the world. If students understood that when they perceive beauty they are being called upon to repair the injuries of the world and to educate themselves, that would be a good thing.

I do think we enter into a relationship with a text, something like what you described in your question. Texts remake us. If I say I am a Keatsian, it means that I read Keats and I have been partly remade by Keats. A made object is always a fulcrum that has magnified benefits beyond the caloric input of the craftsman, and that do not end with a particular reader. Some of these benefits include a greater pliancy of thinking, a greater openness to the concerns of others.

DANIEL GARBER: Derek Attridge raised the question of painting, music, and one could add architecture, all disciplines in which we can talk about reading as well. Reading artifacts in those other contexts may raise ethical questions that are a little different than those raised by the focus on literary texts.

DEREK ATTRIDGE: I think the differences among the modalities of art are easy to exaggerate. Because literature works with language and we use language to talk about it, we all too easily fall into a trap of assuming an exceptionality for the literary work. We do need to think about what it means to read a painting or a building, and so on, and whether it makes sense in those cases to think of what we are doing as trying to divine the intention of the painter or architect or maker. Rather, I think it is in the experience of a viewer or a listener where we should talk about the ethical value of art.

JONATHAN LEAR: We have been talking about the role of literature in making us better, but there are certainly corollary examples of literature making us worse. Literature does not always move us in the direction of the good. We have this idea of the role of literature as deepening the soul, creating inwardness, but readers may become worse off because their ends are bad, not just because they are misreading. Literature can play a role in people becoming extremely mistaken.

ES: I appreciate what you say, and I know there are empirical examples on both sides, but I think the overwhelming effect on people's consciousness is to the good. I know I would need many more examples to convince you, but I do believe it. I suppose I am making an empirical argument, but I am also making a theoretical argument with historical examples.

One more thought—literature and art do this work best when not crowing about their virtues. A lot of the good effects of art work much better when taking a very modest, repudiable position, as the humanities have now in the universities. Universities in the medieval period, and Islamic universities (as George Makdisi has shown[2]), start with the study of poetry and then get to a point where the centrality of that study may get repudiated. I think that is part of the work that literature and art do—that is, they do their work in the world without quite getting their name attached to the effects they have brought about.

ARIANA REILLY: I wanted to make a distinction between reading as such and *producing* readings as critics. In producing or publishing readings and interpretations, it seems that the ethical responsibility lies not in our relationship to an author but actually to our audience. For example, I just heard a paper at a Victorianist conference about a Chartist magazine that, simultaneously while Dickens was being serialized, was reprinting Dickens and removing passages that did not agree with the Chartists, thus presenting Dickens as a Chartist. So that is another instance of promoting one's political goals, perhaps unethically, by distorting or misreading a text.

DA: I agree absolutely that one has multiple responsibilities: to the implied author or creator of the text, but also to one's own auditors and readers, and to one's own historical, political, and social context. These responsibilities are never easily aligned. As Derrida argued in *The Gift of Death*, it is impossible to meet one's responsibilities, and there is bound to be compromise and complication.

JONATHAN CULLER: From my point of view, most of the ethical questions arise not in the reader's relationship to the author, but in one's relationship to one's readers. If you are sitting at home reading, you don't have any responsibility to anyone. That is a moment of freedom. One has the resistances that a work offers to one's initial assumptions, but I don't think there is an ethical cast to that.

II

The Ethics of Reading and the Professions

The Raw and the Half-Cooked

Patricia J. Williams

𝄞 *G-Clef*

I teach a class in Law, Media, and Public Policy. I have a series of images I sometimes show my students with which I play a little game that I call "Caption That Photo." Here's one (Figure 1). Generally, the students look at this and see prayer, pleading, a turning to heaven, supplication.

Here's another (Figure 2). This image too tends to be understood as a scene of supplication and evokes a modicum of sympathy. As a naked visual, there is a sense of desperation, urgency, massive need, an overlay of disaster.

Here's a third image (Figure 3). It is hard to tell, but that thing in the air could be a box of rice being tossed from a ruin. Most of my students see in this unlabeled visual a bucket brigade for vital supplies, survivors excavating not only people from the rubble, but the stuff of life from collapsed stores.

All these pictures are actually taken from the wake of the earthquake in Haiti, as you may have already guessed. The actual titles, as you may also know, are "Looter" for figure 1,[1] "Looters" for figure 2,[2] and "Looters throw a box of goods . . ." for figure 3.[3]

Figure 1.

Figure 2.

Figure 3.

What is interesting is that titles really shift perceptions; if I initially show these images with the captions, the students tend to see riots and lawlessness. So just the word "looter" seems to change the relationship to these figures as legal subjects as well as human beings. The captions redirect attention and channel sympathies quite effectively. So, indeed, upon closer inspection, we can see how frightened that bottle of water must be, how alarmed must be that suspended, airborne box of rice. Indeed, we begin to hear it calling out, "Help, help—I'm being stolen by the greedy undeserving! Rescue me, Uncle Ben, rescue me, the shrink-wrapped embodiment of ordered property relation in an ownership society!"

Hush now . . . Can you hear it? Yes, there, on the breeze . . . the sound of commodities crying?

⑬ *C-Clef*

My subject is the status of that rice: the activity of rice, the intentionality of rice, the miserable, plaintive voice of a ripped-off sack of rice.

I guess another way of putting it is to say that I want to interrogate what gets animated and what does not. How did the humanities become a product rather than a relation? How did we become customers rather than citizens? I am worried about how things live in language and how we objectify in a way that is eventually translated in and into law. For us in the legal academy, the line between human and subhuman, or person and thing, is perpetually urgent, particularly in an era when the limits of incarceration, torture, human trafficking, medical experimentation, and the right to due process often turn on newly minted meanings of words like "enemy combatant," "underclass," "rational actor," "terrorist," or "illegal alien."

And so we ask the ancient questions: What connection do historical taxonomies have to the contemporary perpetuation of sexual servitude, genocide, torture, disappearance, starvation? What disconnections? What about us is truly or essentially "inalienable"? Whom we consider a person as opposed to whom we label as less fully endowed—a corporation? a prisoner?—is a problem that informs some of the most urgent legal and political questions of our time.

All this underscores the large degree of ventriloquism at work in the construction of legal fictions of all sorts, such as standing, legal subjectivity, or personhood. If an egg is "a person" from the instant of fertilization (even in the absence of biological implantation),[4] as asserted by the 2012 Republican Party platform,[5] many of us recognize that it has been endowed by the same mechanisms by which we recognize a municipality or a university or a corporation as a person. When those Republican candidates who have signed the so-called Personhood Amendment invoke "life" in the extremely comprehensive way that they have—including not just fetuses or embryos but the very thought of pregnancy as an immanent theological concept—we might as well call this deployment: imaginary citizens united.

As with the reached-for water bottle or the box of rice, the eternal maternal sanctity of the revived/inspired neo-egg is posited as being in constant battle for its little preborn life with the big, overheated, slutty, sluttish, irrational decision-making moral disregard of a woman who would loot the storehouse of her womb and raid the shelves of innocence.

Consider the voyeuristic "imagineering" of the all-male county commissioners in New Hanover, North Carolina, who turned down funding for a family health clinic while intoning that "if these young women were responsible people and didn't have the sex to begin with, we wouldn't be in this situation." This normalizes some pretty astounding reversals of regard, and makes invisible the hurtful invasiveness of measures like Virginia's attempt to legislate vaginal probes to explore the uncharted geography of women's bodies, to peer and poke around for separate life in there, in need of rescue. Gotta show the selfish thieving hot ungodly babymama enormous, wall-sized visuals of her blastodermic vesicles in case she cannot see, in case she does not know.

In the wake of horrific tragedies like Hurricane Katrina or the earthquake in Haiti, such an objectivizing gaze likewise renders invisible the immediacy of ruination and human need, and rather illuminates the bags of rice and canteens of water and stores of medicine as the exclusive repositories of our protective anxiety and fear. Surely there is a preborn innocent more worthy of their dispensation than these grimy overreachers.

So there is a lexical dimension to being a person in language and the law. It is not a simple matter of whether you are alive or dead. You live or die, you speak or vanish, depending on where you are in the grammatical structure of human events. We are surprised when that rice raises its voice in English, but perhaps we should not be, any more than we are unsurprised when looters are silenced by peacekeeper's gunfire.

When one is a first-class citizen, one is protected by the Bill of Rights and the presumption of innocence and inherent inalienable worth. When one is deemed chattel or an object of private law or an exchange rate in contract, then one is horse-traded and subject to the volatilities of a stock market with only a speculative price that is ever negotiated by others. By the same token, inanimate things can be framed so that they come alive, and live busier, more active lives than flesh, than blood—again, like the corporations in Citizens United,[6] or a worried sack of rice floating above the human chain of starving Haitians.

Think of how much the simple cotton hoodie has assumed agentive properties in relation to the figure of the so-called young black male. The haplessly guileless Geraldo Rivera captured that relation when he said, "The hoodie is as much responsible for Trayvon Martin's death" as George Zimmerman.[7] That living hoodie speaks louder than the flash of deadly gunfire, louder than the figure of the stilled young man.[8] Hence, when Congressman Bobby Rush traded his sober-as-an-undertaker's suit jacket for the loose shroud of a grey hoodie, it did not matter that he was reading a biblical passage about justice and mercy from the book of Micah, chapter 6, verse 8—he and his haberdasheries were quickly hustled out of the chamber by Capitol guards.[9] The interpolated vocality of that hoodie was so fiercely clamorous that it provoked an immediate clamping down of the codes of decorum that prohibited the wearing of hats as per congressional rule 17, clause 5.[10]

"The member is suspended," intoned Gregg Harper, Republican from Mississippi, the impassive presiding officer.[11]

𝄢 F-Clef

Ultimately, this jurisprudential enterprise is centered on what it means to be a person in the eyes of the law—albeit in the figurative eyes of a blind goddess. The germ of this thematic is the Three-Fifths Compromise found in Article I of the Constitution, which apportioned representation by "adding to the whole Number of free Persons, including those bound to Service for a Term of Years, and excluding Indians not taxed, three fifths of all other Persons." By virtue of the institution of slavery, the interrogation of personhood is thus necessarily concerned with race, but the rhetoric of the Constitution broadly engages conceptions of living subjects, legal persons, nonpersons, and personified things.

Perhaps it has always been thus, but the bounds of personhood are being redistricted according to invisible new rules. Americans fear they are in decline, losing ground. We all feel it because these are not the economic times they used to be, but the danger looms that some of us are treating rights as a zero sum game so that whites are being swallowed up by nonwhites, patriarchal order ruined by slovenly, unfaithful women, and money speaks louder than words.[12]

And . . . that hoodies, like burqas, have evolved in this moment of American culture as sites of anxiety and secrecy, as ciphers for honor and betrayal. They provide shelter from hostile gaze yet also the titillation of erotic revelation. They provide a curtain against the world yet speak simultaneously of oppression and indictment and taboo. They chart a tremulous line between person and personification, class and class warfare, animus and eros, between lives constrained by excessive overseeing and deaths made visible by stoning.

So we confront the fluid subjectivity of relation between the visuals of Emmett Till's destroyed, pieced-together body and the smooth, unmarked expanse of Trayvon Martin's nearly intact corpse (but for the tiny efficiencies of bullet address). In either event, the epitaph memorializes a turf-war, a cheap defense of utterly worthless imaginary ground cast as a battle unto death.

⊕ Coda

In her lovely essay "Venus in Two Acts," Saidiya Hartman asks, "how does one rewrite the chronicle of a death foretold and anticipated, as a collective biography of dead subjects, as a counter-history of the human, as the practice of freedom?"[13]

About three weeks after the earthquake, I met a woman at Logan Airport in Boston. She had just arrived from Port-au-Prince, and her story lingers in my mind. We were sitting on a bench waiting for a shuttle bus, and she wanted to talk. She really had to work at sparking that conversation for I was deep in thought and not especially receptive. So it began slowly: She asked about the weather, I answered in monosyllables. She inquired about the timing of the shuttle's arrival, I gave her my copy of the schedule. She kept it going, however, offering small hints of engagement. She was on her way to stay with her son who lived in Rhode Island. "Mmmm," I said. She had three grandchildren. "How nice," I parried. Then she told me where she was coming from, and that she almost had not made it off the island amid all the chaos.

With that, she won my full attention. When I followed her hints and asked the pertinent questions, she fell open, a river of sorrow, a rush of souls, an avalanche of death. So many dead, so many died, she said over and over. She had just gone outside to cook for the family, she lit the fire in the *charbonnière*, the earth shifted, the buildings collapsed. She kept repeating the story: She had been sitting in her yard with the meat half-cooked, the earth shifted for an instant, the buildings collapsed. She told me the same story eight or nine times, each iteration with some new detail: She had seasoned the meat; the flowers were in bloom, her youngest daughter was doing her schoolwork. Then she looked over her shoulder, the earth moved, the house collapsed, and everybody died. All wiped out in the colossal rumbling of an instant.

Suddenly, the woman halted her terrible liturgy, and the story took a turn out of nowhere. "You know what happened," she confided, lowering her voice. "The night before the earthquake there was a funeral for a nine-year-old girl. In the middle of the service, she sat up in her coffin and said 'I'm too hot.' Then she jumped out, ran around the church three times and into the night."

With that, the woman fell silent. She did not speak another word until we parted.

"Here is a story," my grandmother used to begin her best tales, "that is and isn't true." And that is how I came to hear this woman's tale, this story straight from the book of the dead or the day of the dead, or, as my grandmother used to describe it, the night that has no eyes. Wombs and tombs tumbling open, the earth stalked by ghosts. For everything else she said that might have been accepted as factual, it was that supernatural image of the little girl rising from her coffin that brought home the horror and incalculable fear of the hellish night in Port-au-Prince—the bodies never found by families who remain nameless, the disorder that will bend and break an entire generation, the losses that will not be recorded nor find their way to collective address, into the consciousness we call history—all the incomprehensible reversals of logic and illogic, the quick and the moribund, the active and the passive.

Once I began to hear her story as parable, it had a perfect coherence: It pointed to the enormity of that hole in time when the laws of man and nature had turned upsidedown so that the dead became alive and the alive became dead, even as they were preparing to eat. That conjuration conveyed more vividly than all the political, media, and statistical accounts combined what she had encountered when she had gone out into the evening, and she had prepared the fire, and the meat was half-cooked, and the building collapsed.

Conquering the Obstacles to Kingdom and Fate: The Ethics of Reading and the University Administrator

Ralph J. Hexter (with Craig Buckwald)

Like the poet of the *Aeneid*, I come to sing of troubles and challenges, formidable ones, even beyond our expectation, and so I might join Virgil in asking, incredulously, "Can there be such anger in the hearts of the gods" ("Tantaene animis caelestibus irae?" *Aeneid* 1.33)? I cite Virgil for a number of reasons, not least because it takes me back to my familiar haunts as a classicist. A long interpretive tradition has seized on Virgil as a poet who, especially in the *Aeneid*, focuses on showing how difficult it can be to follow an ethical course for those who are looked upon to lead, but also how important it is. This last point, especially as it applies to my own professional position of university leader, is the focus of my essay.

It is well and good for us to come together in this symposium to affirm the importance of reading ethically and to explore how the humanities might play a key role in removing this practice from the endangered species list. I thank Peter and all of the organizers and participants for making this symposium possible, and also express my admiration for the noble motive behind it; I am hopeful that it will have an impact. Let me begin by describing four challenges that are faced by a university leader who desires and attempts to read ethically.

Challenge 1: The Epistemological Problem of Ethical Understanding

When we think about the practice of reading *unethically*, I suspect that most of us first conceive a moral failing—an embrace of or surrender to the dark side. This is the charge that Mercury levels at Aeneas when, visiting him in the lap of love and luxury in Carthage, he says Aeneas is "forgetful of [his] kingdom and fate," or "affairs" ("Regni rerumque oblite tuarum!" *Aeneid* 4.267).

But we must consider an alternative scenario of not being forgetful, but unable to see—because it is an elementary lesson of ethics that the best course is not always clear to us. In fact, rather than having to choose between an ethical and an unethical course of action, we often are faced with a number of potentially conflicting choices, each of which makes a valid claim to being ethical. In other words, we face an epistemological problem. Probably the best-known example of the difficulty of determining the right ethical course involves the potential conflict between deontological and consequentialist ethical perspectives—that is, one holding that we must be ethical in our actions and the other maintaining that the ends justify the means.

The value of this sort of parsing can be seen in how it helps us to understand the so-called Torture Memos that are one motivation for our gathering. In his reading of the Constitution and international law in the memos, John Yoo maintains he was an honest and accurate reader, even though there is little doubt that the ends that his reading served have helped to define his reading's ethical status. It is clear that some of those who support Professor Yoo's reading see it as honest and accurate, if also disturbing; others see it as violating honest reading in the service of a another all-important principle, sometimes called "national security." It is my belief that a conflict of ethical perspectives, rather than brazenly unethical conduct, is chiefly responsible for the enduring controversy surrounding the memos. But let me be clear: Sometimes we are right to regard someone as a villain, regardless of how the villain views himself or herself.

As I have mentioned, for this panel on "The Ethics of Reading and the Professions," I draw on my experience as a professional of sorts—a university administrator, specifically, provost of the University of California, Davis—but it is as a professor in the humanities that I reflect on the challenges of my current office. Again, there is a valid parallel to be drawn between my position as provost and that of Professor Yoo when he worked in the Department of Justice's Office of Legal Counsel. In both cases, the office holders are often asked to "read"—in the sense of publicly interpret—various texts in order to support a leadership function. In the case of the university administrator, this reading is performed on foundational texts, such as a state constitution or an institution's mission statement; dialogical texts, such as task force reports or scientific studies; and the real-world texts of current or historical events. Being pulled in different directions by two or more ethical claims is at the heart of these types of administrative reading. Let me cite a couple of cases from my own institution.

The first has to do with our campus task force on the Native American Graves Protection and Repatriation Act (NAGPRA). The task force was recently reactivated in order to provide advice to the university on new regulations addressing the possession of "culturally unidentifiable remains"—that is, remains not linked to a federally recognized tribe according to certain definable protocols. Many remains so classified are currently in the possession of the Davis campus and other University of California campuses.

In reading NAGPRA and the new regulations, I recognize the validity of a number of different and potentially conflicting ethical imperatives: to be an honest and accurate reader of a federal law; to serve the Native American tribes that have strong cultural connections to the remains in question and remains in general; to look after the university's interests in the matter, which are also in large part the interests of historical and ethnographic research; and even to preserve and foster a harmonious relationship among the Davis campus (some of whose students, faculty, and staff are Native American), Native American tribes near and far, and the people of California. The situation is further complicated by the fact that the interests of the different stakeholders are thoroughly interrelated, and serving one interest often serves another as well, though passionate advocacy may obscure this.

The second case I wish to cite has to do with the reading of a document known as the California Master Plan for Higher Education, whose original version was written in 1960. The Master Plan is an ambitious scheme for public higher education in California that designates distinct roles for the University of California system, the state university system, and the community college system. But the Plan is better known as a formal expression of California's promise of educational opportunity. As such, the document specifies the percentages of top high school graduates that the University of California system will admit.

In reading the Master Plan, the administrator is pulled in at least two directions: toward both a literalist reading that respects the original admit goal and a looser reading that accommodates a modification of the goal for practical reasons. Both readings, it might be said, have ethical justification. This example is especially important because at its heart is one of the most important ethical questions facing public higher education today: How does one divide resources between students and the university at large? Or, to put it differently, how do we balance the goal of maintaining broad educational opportunity with the goal of advancing institutional excellence (especially as the latter is perceived nationally and internationally)? As we saw with NAGPRA, the ethical situation here is all the more tangled in that directing resources to one entity may potentially, if sometimes indirectly, benefit the other as well.

Challenge 2: Corporate Reading

The second challenge to the administrator who desires and attempts to read ethically has to do with being part of a university structure. It is a reality of large and complex organizations, such as major research institutions, that a top administrator, alone, has neither the time nor the requisite knowledge and expertise to give an adequate reading for larger audiences of all of the written and real-world texts that come his or her way. For this reason, a leader typically practices what I will call "corporate reading," which I use in a neutral rather than nefarious sense (that is, one referencing for-profit corporations) to designate "shared interpretive labor." Let me cite one more case from my institution.

The relationship between the First Amendment and campus protests was of urgent concern on the Davis campus for several months after the collective trauma of the pepper spray incident of November 18, 2011. This concern intensified with subsequent protests against a bank branch on our campus and also with an event at which two Israelis, one a soldier, spoke on campus amid significant disruptions.

As provost, I have found it necessary to "read" the First Amendment and related law to various campus and public audiences. But being neither a constitutional scholar nor an attorney, I incorporated into my reading that of the university's general counsel, but not solely his, because for all his general legal expertise there are others—for example, professors at our law school and the law school dean—who have even greater specialized knowledge of constitutional law and greater credibility with faculty, students, and much of the public. In fact, as is typically the case, my readings of the First Amendment are the products of a rather larger group of individuals at the university, with different areas of expertise and at different levels. It is truly a collaborative effort. This is not only a necessary way of proceeding, but also arguably a more ethically responsible one: The process is designed to keep someone from saying more than he or she knows.

On the other hand, corporate reading undoubtedly presents challenges to ethical reading. For example, whenever I cite or paraphrase a colleague, administrative or professorial, I believe but cannot be absolutely certain that he or she has fully complied with the ethical responsibilities of due diligence and honesty. But in the absence of some sort of red flag, and after exercising reasonable testing, it is my job to trust in my colleague's contributions and utilize them as needed. As a result, my provostial readings—ones that are presented under my name and administrative office—may inadvertently mask another's ethical transgressions. This matters because, in such a case, my readings might further legitimize untruths or bad-faith analyses and thereby facilitate bad institutional decisions. My perception is that various control mechanisms, formal and informal, have prevented such pernicious elements from afflicting my provostial readings, but this structural vulnerability must be acknowledged.

Corporate reading also presents a second challenge to ethical reading, one that is perhaps more powerful and more frequently encountered. Because it divides interpretive labor among numerous individuals, corporate reading can more easily allow an individual's ethical awareness to slip between the cracks, get lost in the shuffle, or simply be eclipsed by the immensity of the process itself. In a worst-case scenario, corporate reading can foster a myopia in which institutional interests, narrowly defined, are placed above higher principles, the university's true mission, or the real interests of those that the institution is intended to serve.

Challenge 3: Conflicting Subject Matter, Conflicting Technologies of Reading

The third challenge to ethical reading that I wish to cite addresses the chief hypothesis of this panel, if not the entire symposium, namely that ethical reading in the professions can be fostered by importing humanities training and knowledge into the public realm. The argument for the humanities as a key to promoting ethical reading can be stated, with extreme reduction, as something like this: Humanities training and knowledge make us more skilled readers as well as more ethical individuals.

Clearly, as stated, our hypothesis seems to rest on the dubious assumption that the humanities are, for important intents and purposes, homogenous. It assumes, alarmingly, a sufficient identity of content and practice throughout the disciplines that are grouped under the name "humanities." This is problematic for more important reasons than the fact that the list of humanities disciplines often varies from one institution to the next. The heart of the problem is that there are many differences in subject matter and practice across the different humanities disciplines that we have every reason to suspect may, most often if not always, produce significantly different reading abilities and practices, different sensibilities and dispositions, and possibly even different sorts of people. Indeed, given the great variation among corresponding departments at different institutions and even among the faculty in a single department, the heterogeneity seems to run very deep. All of this is to say that when we imagine saving the species of ethical reading by bringing the humanities into the public realm, it is far from clear what product we contemplate importing.

This is not the place for me to attempt to explore in any comprehensive way *how* the heterogeneity that pervades the humanities bears on their ability to foster ethical reading, though the topic surely deserves further exploration. Instead, let me just share a question about my own primary field, literature.

I wonder if it makes a difference to our overall ethical capacity and behavior if our literary knowledge and training skew more toward so-called traditionalist or old reading and its favoring of the canon, or toward newer, more theoretically informed varieties and their greater willingness both to venture beyond the canon and to ask rather different questions of texts. The debate over new and old reading, which is now largely passé, centered on passionate claims about the difference one's affiliation would make in accurate reading—and often in one's ethical awareness and character. Although we must avoid making easy assumptions about correlations between a reader's ethics and what or how he or she reads, the existence of those correlations—weak or powerful—seems at least plausible. Not to admit this would be to maintain that different interpretive practices and literary texts, each of which can be said to provide a unique ethical education, do not also possibly shape ethical awareness and values in unique ways. At least in our present state of ignorance, this is an unsupportable position, I would say. I will return to this subject a little later.

Challenge 4: Ethical Courage

The final challenge is the one touched upon at the beginning of my talk, when I referred to Aeneas's difficult decision between a life of ease in Carthage with Dido, and the punishing but god-ordained fate of founding Rome. Dido accuses Aeneas of having a hard heart. But sensitive reading, I think, suggests not an unfeeling hero but rather a hero struggling and succeeding in making his heart hard once he realizes his ethical duty. Within the framework of Roman *pietas*, his duty is not only to the gods but also to his father Anchises, his son Ascanius, and the people who follow him, for the quality of their future is at stake along with Roman greatness. My point is a commonplace: It is often extremely difficult to follow the ethical course even after one identifies it. But I make this point anyway because, for all I can tell, the modern individual is very adept at rationalizing unethical behavior—behavior that, without certain inducements or pressures, he or she would readily identify as unethical.

One might counter that the practice of cleverly excusing the inexcusable has a long history, a fact powerfully reflected in many canonical texts. Think Milton's Satan, Shakespeare's Iago, the Callicles of Plato's *Gorgias*, or the Odysseus of Sophocles's *Philoctetes*. In the sixth century B.C.E., Theognis of Megara was already lamenting the decline of ethics as wealth and individualism rose. My goodness, we can go back to Cain and his "primal eldest" murder and rationalization.

Although I am not able to resolve this question about how the modern period may or may not differ from earlier ones with respect to rationalizing unethical behavior, all is not lost. My main concern is not to establish that this pathology is uniquely modern, but rather to acknowledge that it is currently flourishing. Yet it might also profit us to consider how the unique conditions of our historical moment—including but not limited to the growth and influence of professional specialization, so-called corporate culture, and public relations practices—may be especially nurturing of that pathology, or at least of its current forms.

So far in this essay, I have focused on challenges, all of them formidable and complex. Before I conclude, let me at least attempt to do something that administrators aspire to do: *problem solve*. Once again, I call your attention to the *Aeneid*. Before Mercury's wake-up call, Aeneas had a plan to take a sort of middle course, to be able to enjoy love and luxury in North Africa while at the same time honoring his destiny to found Rome. He would do this by building a joint empire with Dido in Carthage. In the same way, all of us have powerful motivation and great capacity to avoid ethical imperatives.

But Aeneas—as Virgil constructed him for an Augustan audience and from an unavoidable Augustan perspective, which was perforce post–Punic Wars—came to see that there was no middle course that would serve both desire and duty. In the same way, I believe that we must get better at making difficult choices regarding our ethical behavior, and I have a few suggestions for university leaders with respect to reading.

In Reading, the Ends Do Not Justify the Means

As readers—that is, as interpreters—we should skew deontological as Odysseus strategically steered nearer Scylla than Charybdis, on his first pass at least, minimizing his losses. That is to say, we should be ethical in our process rather than use ends to justify unethical means. I say this because, if we cannot be relied upon to read in good faith, with accuracy and without ulterior motive, the solid ground of truth is lost in our larger discourse, and our communities become fragmented and acrimonious. These are costs that even ostensibly enlightened institutions such as universities have grown comfortable paying, at least from time to time. But they are too dear.

But what, you may say, about our responsibility to keep an eye on the future, on making sure that our reading will produce ends that are beneficial to the communities we serve? Fortunately, there is a way for the administrator to fulfill that duty too, as an executive, which includes both decision making and advocating for certain policies. The well-rounded administrator must be both an ethical reader and a competent executive, performing the duties of both according to the trust that the public has placed in him or her.

Regarding the Challenges of Corporate Reading and the Heterogeneity of the Humanities

I have said that one danger of corporate reading is the development of a myopia that puts the interests of the institution, narrowly defined, ahead of higher principles, the university's true mission, or the interests of those the institution is intended to serve. An argument in favor of this myopia is that the institution must be served if it is to survive and do anyone any good. There is some force to this argument, but its invocation should always be regarded with a healthy skepticism—for, in essence, it is a trickle-down argument that may promise general benefits that never materialize.

Regarding which reading technologies to apply, as administrators we should keep an eye on what our duty is to the varied constituency that we serve, and how well suited a technology is to fulfilling that duty. Given that an administrator is expected to communicate clearly and honestly to individuals who have very different backgrounds and areas of expertise, he or she should attempt to speak in a generally accessible language of words and concepts. At the same time, and for obvious reasons, the administrator's reading should concentrate on topics and issues that are of concern to the general public. Finally, the administrator should read the whole truth in the sense of addressing all that his or her reading pretends to address—in other words, all that is relevant and important. I would also urge the exercise of the practice of "interpretive charity," by which I mean striving to read a text—whether written or "real world"—with fairness, respect, and at least an initial working assumption that it contains or may lead to wisdom that the reader presently lacks.

Although the administrative reading I am describing may seem more traditionalist than not, it will ill serve its proper purpose—and its public—if it does not avail itself of some of the skeptical, demystifying, and even deconstructive techniques regarded as of more recent vintage. I do not believe this joining of traditionalist and nontraditionalist reading practices means producing some monstrous, Minotaur-like hybrid. Indeed, I think I could make the case that the aforementioned new techniques have much in common with the old ones. An important example is the Socratic *elenchus*.[1] But I would also draw your attention to moves that blunt and parry the thrust of such clever critical attacks—for example, the almost perversely literal reading of Caesar's coin with which Jesus confutes the Pharisees' entrapping questions about taxation.[2]

But the date of our reading techniques is not the issue, nor is the date of the real-world or written texts upon which we use them. If we want to promote ethical reading in the professions, our attention is better directed toward gaining a deeper understanding of how different sorts of texts and reading practices help to shape our ethical awareness and values. Only then will we be able to make a reasonable appraisal of *what* in that vast and heterogeneous world called the "humanities" we should work to import into the public realm. Having said this, I will add that I have personally known humanities scholars of every field and theoretical persuasion who have had great success in furthering the ethical education of their students.

Responses and Discussion

Richard Sennett

I would like to make two brief comments, one on the beginning of Patricia Williams's essay and the other on the question of professional education and the humanities from the view of somebody who is more involved in the profession of urban design and planning than literature itself.

Williams's essay is really remarkable. It is particularly striking to me because I was in Haiti a few months ago, and I will share something with you that amazed me. There are 13,000 aid organizations in Haiti at the moment, and they are getting very little accomplished. One of the reasons is that a lot of the aid depends on people being considered "worthy recipients" of the aid—that is, not being in any way prosecuted or identified as looters. So because this was a situation of mass need in which there was very little that people could get, especially in the first fourteen weeks after the earthquake, large numbers of people have been disempowered by this label.

What struck me about Williams's presentation is that it raises a profound question about the act of naming images. What has happened with her students looking at these images—and with many of the Haitian aid agencies—is that the relation between word and image becomes one in which the word exerts power by naming the *agent* rather than the *action*. The labeling of *who* is in the image becomes the interpretation of *what* the image is about. That is a radical way of restricting the publicness of images and how we understand their public value by essentially assigning the value to who they are, rather than what they are doing. It shrinks the room for interpretation about *why* they are doing what they are doing because they are identified in terms of the agent acting. This is a phenomenon of public life in general, that when we reduce ambiguity by erasing the question of an unknown agent and replacing it with a known agent—and in this case a stigmatized one—the actual consideration of what they are doing diminishes. This is a profound diminution of the public realm.

When I look at the image of the box of rice in the air with all these hands stretched out, what strikes me is that there is just one box. The reason their hands are stretched out has to do with the near starvation conditions in Haiti. The fact that they are "looters" is irrelevant. So we want to focus on the box of rice as an emblem that creates a terrain for the discussion of what the situation is there, rather than on the question of agents, of who is doing what. By the way, I think the proper name for the action in the photo in Williams' paper is "supplication."

This is a huge discussion now, ironically, for people at Google, who are in the process of assembling an enormous library of photographic images. What has struck them is that the labeling technique they use—which is to identify *who* is in the photo—means that the public usage of the photos diminishes compared with when they try to categorize the activities in the photos. That is, the act of identifying the actors leads to less use of the images than if a more difficult categorization were used, having to do with naming action. So this problem raised in Williams's paper has many dimensions.

I also want to say something about the humanities in the professional realm from the perspective of someone who has had more contact with architects and engineers, particularly in the work I do on cities, than with humanists proper. It is an observation about the use that the humanities have been put to in these kinds of technical realms.

What I have observed is founded on the notion that any good technical craftsman needs also to be imaginative. Technical craftwork that is just problem solving is a kind of low-level activity. In places like the Massachusetts Institute of Technology or the California Institute of Technology, there are reasons they have active music and literature departments—they are elements in the development of good craftsmanship. But those are elite institutions. When you get lower down the pecking order of institutional prestige, this kind of reaching out to the humanities on the part of people doing technical work diminishes. It has a very complex framing to it. In part, it is that at a state school of planning or engineering, people's realistic assessment is that the jobs they are going to get depend purely on technical expertise, but it is more than that. In the United States, technical work is distributing itself such that people who come from high-status, high-prestige institutions are given more freedom to be fully creative, to be craftsmen, to imagine possibilities, to be problem *finders* rather than problem solvers. The atmosphere in this elite technical realm privileges the asking of interpretive questions.

So, to me, when I look at this issue about the humanities in technical education, what I see is an issue of inequality that has to do with professional life in the technical realm rather than the question of whether the humanities are valuable. It really has to do with the world of professional training becoming so unequal that only the people at the top believe there is some opportunity for them to be fully good craftspeople and engage in humanistic pursuits. I am told the same inequality exists at business schools. What I am suggesting in conclusion is that we may have this turned around a little: The problem is not whether the humanities are valuable, but to whom they are valuable. And that difference depends on a profound and growing inequality on the technical side of university life.

Michael Roth

THE AVOIDANCE OF READING

I have given my response a title, "The Avoidance of Reading," with a wink to the philosopher Stanley Cavell, whose essay on *King Lear*, "The Avoidance of Love," has been so important to me ever since I was a student.

It is odd to be back at Princeton for this symposium. I came here in 1978 as a graduate student. At that time, many people were very interested in violent reading, playful reading, the pleasure of reading, disruptive reading, turning things inside out, and finding a good pun. Now we are interested in the ethics of reading, and I have been asking myself whether this is progress or something else.

When we turn to ethics, what are we trying to avoid? This panel is entitled "The Ethics of Reading and the Professions." Its description says,

"Professional education may be the most characteristic and powerful product of the modern American University." I am the president of Wesleyan University, and we do not have any professional schools. In this regard, we are closer to Princeton than to the other Ivy League research universities. But even understanding the important economic and professional role of the professional schools at other American universities, I would not have supposed that this was our most distinctive national feature. In the past, the American university's continued support for liberal education has been our most characteristic and powerful product. This has meant support for an education that leads only to more education: inquiry for the sake of inquiry.

But I realize professional education at universities *is* powerful. From where I sit, in a school that focuses on undergraduate education, I can still see professionalization in the humanities and the social sciences, and, of course, in the sciences. You do not need a medical school or a business school to have professionalization. Many on our faculty seem to hunger for professionalization, even as they mock it; and that mockery has become more and more esoteric ("professional"), only available to those in the guild. One of the worst features of even so-called interdisciplinary work in the humanities since the 1960s is professionalization. To speak baldly, professionalization at the university is driven by envy, money, and the fear of ambiguity. Pride in strong departments capable of luring people away from other strong departments is its most obvious but not most important symptom.

First, in response to Ralph Hexter's essay, I do not believe there are noninstrumental administrative ways of reading. I always look for my wallet whenever I hear about noninstrumental administrative anything, because bureaucratic instrumentality can never be noninstrumental. I think the bureaucratization of the university, of which I am a part, is a horrible feature of university life. I can sleep at night (sometimes) because I think, being part of that bureaucratic instrumentality, I preserve the possibility for my colleagues to do the wonderful work that people are doing in conferences like this.

I do not think there is an epistemological problem for ethical understanding. I would borrow from Ian Hacking and Michel Foucault in saying that, in regard to ethical matters, deciding what counts as ethical substance is a process in which there is no truth of the matter. You decide what community you are going to have allegiance to, or you find yourself in one. Then you figure out how you participate in that community; you find ways of belonging, or of excluding yourself.

In regard to Patricia Williams's paper, I was intrigued and stimulated by the project of interrogating what gets animated and what does not. Pointing out who gets to count for us, who gets to count for the law, and how it has come to be that way is an important task. Pointing out who gets excluded in this process is an urgent task. Williams's final recounting of the Haitian woman's story invites us to let more count for us. I do not know if that is ethical, but in my community it is a very good thing to do.

I have a few concluding comments. First, from violent reading to ethics, what are we afraid of, what are we trying to avoid? I think Jonathan Culler said it very well: We have been accused of nihilism for so long that many seemed to feel that we had to come up with some way of appealing to the instrumentalism around us. Ethics might be the least bad way of doing that, but I am not sure. However, in appealing to ethics—that is, in appealing not just to the ethics of reading but also to a kind of aesthetic experience that would make us ethical—I have a hard time understanding what to do with the potential ethical value of other imaginative activities. Take the ethics of watching television, for example. I do not know whether watching television is more or less ethical than reading, but I think all of us would find it odd to believe that we are becoming, as a culture, better people, more empathetic, or more capable of imagining others because of television or because of YouTube. Why would reading be ethically superior as a genre of experience?

Finally, what are we trying to do, or not do, when we move from playful or violent and disruptive reading to ethics? I sense a fear of reading here. Reading may lead nowhere; we may get lost in reading. For those of us in the humanities, feeling this loss, the pleasure of being lost, has been an important practice, sometimes even a goal—even an opiate, as Elaine Scarry has called it. In reading, we may feel ourselves exposed. We may feel the shame or the delight in our own ungroundedness. Whether one takes as one's model of reading Jane Addams's sympathetic interpretations or Jacques Derrida's deconstruction, through reading we apprehend that things could—that we could—be otherwise. I do not think that means that we will be (ethically) better, but it does mean that we can imagine being otherwise.

When we turn to ethics, what are we are trying to avoid? We are trying, I think, to avoid reading because reading, to recall the Torture Memos referred to in the invitation to this conference, *makes nothing impossible.* If we can agree that reading leads us to be lost, leads to ungroundedness, then we must admit that we do not find in reading as such any way of rejecting the Torture Memos. We *can* reject torture, but that is not an ethics of reading but politics—that is, a struggle for power.

Reading leaves us exposed, as Cavell has said, or it leaves us, as Derrida has said, in the undecidable. Those running from studies based in reading to studies based in numbers or systems are often running from ambiguity and its exposures. And an appeal to progress, whether historical or ethical, seems to me another effort to reduce that ambiguity. I would ask that we not join the rush from reading by trying to contain its ambiguity with a label like ethics.

William Germano

This session presented two essays pertaining to the formulation "the ethics of reading and the professions." What procedures or protocols would govern something as decisive and lofty as an "ethics of reading," and what specific gravity attaches to the more earthborn "the ethics of reading *and* (ah, the copula) *the professions*"? Given our contributors and my distinguished fellow respondents, it seems most useful to me to ground my own participation in the experience of my first career, almost thirty years long, as an academic publisher, at Routledge and at Columbia, before I came to Cooper Union.

PROFESSIONS

Let me begin with the leading term "the professions." The traditional concept of the professions is an old one, perhaps now too old to be useful. My inquiry to the Online Oxford English Dictionary concerning the word *professions* yielded the response "Try again," which may be telling us something about the nature of professionalism at this moment.

A search for the singular term *profession*, on the other hand, generates a list of meanings reaching back to the early thirteenth century, where its sense of "declaration, promise, or vow" is directly related to entering religious orders. Professions are demonstrations of faith, and so bound in an originary sense to moral commitment. In his great essay "Nature" (1836), Emerson would describe ethics as "a system of human duties commencing from man," rather than from God. Professions and ethics are already bound to one another. The sense of human duty is central to what we as professors do, and that thing that we do we do professionally.

As a college teacher, I train professionals. At Cooper Union, every student is in a four- or five-year undergraduate professional program in art, architecture, or engineering. We have no liberal arts majors. Each class is likely to be that student's only undergraduate exposure to philosophy or musicology or economics or Shakespeare. What we think of here as ethical reading—patient, critical, attentive, and deeply humane—sounds like close reading meets Second Corinthians. It is a good platform, and not only for young, highly focused students already eager to pursue professional lives.

The commercial business of publishing is not a profession like law or medicine, much less clergy. But the practice of reading is so centrally dependent upon the work that publishing undertakes—the work of selection, development, and dissemination—that publishing is, it seems to me, inescapably written into the question of ethics. Selection, development, and dissemination are what universities do with the students in their charge, and what we as teachers are pledged to undertake.

There are many kinds and forms of publishing, each with its own ethical dilemmas and failures: from the idealistic (as in the debates over free and open access) to the particular (as in the delimitations of ownership and liability in relation to what seems increasingly to be called "academic work product"), on down to the sad and scandalous (as in the phone-hacking episode that brought down a British newspaper). Regarded somewhere between a "profession" and a "trade," publishing is nevertheless central to reading and to the ethical questions that engage us at this symposium. I will return in a moment to the question of writing.

Whether we like it or not, the humanities are burdened with a dual charge and mixed messages. The first descends from the market and demands self-justification. *Why the humanities at all? Why now?* Yet there is still a second demand, a demand for answers arising from the ongoing curiosity concerning the human condition, a demand that we provide tools for understanding the human experience. It is the thing we guard, reinvent, and supply to each generation and to each class of persons. It is what makes ordinary adults want to turn on the news or browse Wikipedia or even read the *Aeneid.* And it is what turns otherwise reasonable young people into majors in humanistic disciplines.

Our dual charge contains contradictory postures, one resentful, one needy and curious. American society's cultural response to the humanities, even at its most sympathetic, is *odi et amo:* I hate you, and I love you. In society's least sympathetic mode, the humanities seem more like Philoctetes (to whom Ralph Hexter alludes briefly), repellent but essential to the social project. If we cannot easily answer this contradictory outcry, we can at least focus on what we do and why. For the question of an "ethics of reading"—and especially an "ethics of reading *and the professions*"—is finally a question of practice.

READING

Is reading a stage in Robert Darnton's communication circuit? A means of delivering information? An interpretative act? The two essays in this section shape the discussion of the ethics of reading in very different ways. Despite the framing gesture toward Virgil in Ralph Hexter's paper, neither he nor Patricia Williams addresses narrowly literary concerns, which is a good thing. Hexter's paper counsels that in reading we should "skew deontological"; in his "challenges to ethical reading," he wisely singles out what he calls "corporate reading," though deploying the term, as he puts it, "in a neutral rather than nefarious sense" in order to define "shared interpretive labor."

As administrators know, humanists are perhaps the least likely academics to see themselves as participants in shared interpretive labor. Most of us persist in sustaining the vision of single-author creation, even when we know that shared interpretive labor might yield a superior result. Professional reading in the humanities is attentive, suspicious, and frequently lonely; our systems of reward continue to valorize what is fundamentally a deformation of heroic individualism, long after the last Romantic poet was laid to rest among the daffodils. We think we want to do it (whatever *it* is) alone.

Given the humanist distrust of anything with the word "corporate" attached to it, I was particularly struck by Hexter's repositioning of "corporate reading" within the campus community. The kinds of reading we all do, but especially those of us in administrative positions, are, it seems to me, inescapably examples of shared interpretive labor. But I would add that the mechanism of scholarly publishing is also always an example of both corporate reading (in a literal sense) and "shared intellectual labor." University presses and scholarly journals have so internalized a set of collective reading practices that those involved sometimes forget how much sharing does, in fact, take place.

Williams's essay, delivered in her signature writing voice, is a reminder of the agency of images and of their immense textual power. In calling our attention to the sentence structure of human events, she reminds us further that, for better or worse, we think about the world through language. "There is a lexical dimension to being a person in language and the law," she writes. So an ethics of reading is needed to set the terms within which not just documents but persons and human events can be read right.

Consequential Interpretation

The work of ethical reading is supposed to be many things—conscious, critical, humane, patient, attentive. These are all good things, and we would like our engineers and doctors, our information technology specialists and waitstaff, our parents and children, our teachers and even our politicians to be able to decipher the world's complex messages. But we also want—and deserve—more from one another than momentary, disposable attention. We want our ethical readers to be changed somehow, to experience an ethically interpretive reading as liberating or troubling so that reading becomes consequential—compelling and important in a dynamic sense, leaving the reader altered.

As both Williams's and Hexter's papers demonstrate, reading has consequences. No form of reading can or should escape the act of interpretation, and every act of interpretation has the potential to be generative. A provost's memo (as in Hexter's example) or a photo caption (as Williams demonstrates) will yield interpretation and further texts, in a process that can go on and on until the textual event is exhausted. In this sense, ethical reading is not only what we want to do all the time but a praxis collaborative with its subject. As Gerald Graff says of writing pedagogy, when we teach writing we ask bluntly of the student's written work, "OK, so what?"[1] When I work with professional writers—primarily professors—outside my institution, I ask the same question concerning their work in progress. To observe, to interpret, this is what professors do: We notice things. But if the gesture extends no further, the circuit remains incomplete. There have to be consequences of interpretation so that ethical reading—can we speak of any other kind?—does not congratulate itself on being pure. Reading and interpretation are the beginning of intellectual, social, and political work. Ethical reading is smart, clean, fair and square, but only if it produces consequential interpretation—not the deliverables against which Judith Butler cautions us, but an *outcome* with the potential to change the world, the text, and the reader.

I will conclude by joining the world of publishing to the professions, and ethical reading to the ethical responsibility of writing. The act of reading ethically, which is to say reading both the lexical construct and the social text, must remind us that ethical *writing* is a duty beyond questions of truth value, systematic method, and full citation. Ethical writing is propelled by a sense of obligation to unknowable readers. If all reading involves the act of interpretation, then writing must be cognizant of its own interpretability. To write with care—and with as much clarity as contentions will support—in turn enables readerly interpretation. The ability to write well is a developable skill, and to write with courage and clarity is to honor the reader, which is the beginning of ethical engagement in any field, any profession. The world is composed of stories true and untrue, as Williams reminds us, and those stories are doled out in the language of which we are the stewards. The ethics of that seems pretty clear to me: Write as if you mean it, and write as if what you write can change the reader. Because it will.

Discussion Session 2: The Ethics of Reading and the Professions

PETER BROOKS: I want to start us off with the point Bill Germano made, that some kinds of reading are by their nature consequential. For instance, people are tortured as a result. Jane Mayer has made the argument that the Bush administration began by perverting language, and that everything else came in the wake of that. I am not sure whether I agree, but it certainly is true that if you pervert language there is no longer any way to establish what *is* an ethical reading.

MICHAEL ROTH: I don't think torture and murder are consequences of the perversion of language. Obviously, I think the fight against torture is important, but it is misguided to try to give the humanities importance by saying that a better trained, humanistically minded lawyer—that is, a lawyer who would agree with us and our political values—would have been less likely to defend torture. The problem was the desire to pursue a war strategy at any cost, not that the education of the lawyer was not humanistic enough. In other words, I think the problem is political, and I don't see why some formal notion of a more ethical reading would save us in a political struggle against those people who want to use torture in order to enhance national security or their own power.

JUDITH BUTLER: Michael, I thought you were saying that a memo in itself does not act. What a text says is one thing, and then the actions that may or may not follow are another. But it does seem to me that certain kinds of memos are speech acts with perlocutionary consequences. If you are a law professor or government lawyer and you write this memo, and your standing will confer legitimacy on torture, then you are not just writing a text rather than doing a thing. The text is a speech act with consequences, and the consequences are amplified under certain conditions; that is, there is a government looking for legal justification for torture, and you are professionally qualified to pass judgment on how to read relevant legal texts and laws. I can't see that we can say that torture is wrong but the memo authorizing it is not.

MR: I am not suggesting that the Torture Memos were not wrong. But the problem is the torture and the issue of the techniques of reading that led to those memos are less important than the political imperative to produce torture. I don't think an education in the kind of reading we would approve of is the most important goal to strive for in trying to eliminate the possibilities of government-sanctioned torture.

JB: I don't think the question is a technique of reading. I think a technique of reading could go either way or serve different purposes. I think the ethics of reading is a question of for whom and for what do we read, and in the service of what kind of world. Perhaps we do need to question where torture does begin and end. We can be positivist and say that it begins when the hand is raised to inflict it, but it does have an institutional and cultural history. We do have a role in either stoking or deflating that legitimacy effect.

MR: What if we just said it is a politics of reading instead of an ethics of reading? What if we said that the politics of reading in the Torture Memos is nefarious?

RICHARD SENNETT: It is the acceptance of the memos as legitimate that is the problem. We want to make readers more skeptical, and in order for them to be more skeptical they need to be more skilled in getting behind technical or abstract language. Surely the politics of reading lies in enabling readers to translate what is often hidden behind technical language. It is a skill that has to be learned. It is a question of whether you can empower people to read more critically, especially in this country where we are orientated to believe in professional expertise.

MR: I think that inflates the importance of what we do as teachers of reading.

JONATHAN LEAR: I want to offer an anecdote that relates to Judith's comment. As a freshman at Yale, I was trying out for the *Yale Daily News* and my first assignment was to cover a story about alleged physical branding of initiates at a fraternity. I called up the president of this fraternity, whose name was George W. Bush. Obviously, I didn't know then that I was interviewing the future president. In fact, I forgot all about this until George W. Bush was running for president and a reporter from the *New Haven Register* contacted me and asked if I had written this article. I got a copy of the article, and I found it to be uncanny in two ways. First, Bush said then what he said for the rest of his career, which was, basically, "It's not as bad as you think." But second, and this really stood out, I had gotten a quote from an associate dean who said, in effect, that boys will be boys, that Yale will let them settle it themselves. This is the kind of thoughtless sanctioning of the act we have been talking about. What if that dean had responded to this issue with indignation, requiring a public conversation about this kind of behavior? How might history have been different? What if Bush's education had included such an intervention? By the way, the dean was also probably a man who appreciated reading and could give an excellent lecture about the value of the humanities.

JONATHAN ARAC: I am struck by this exchange on the question of politics and the practice of close or analytic reading, and want to offer an historical perspective. One of the motives for I. A. Richards's work in the 1920s, which is foundational for this conversation, was the widely shared belief that the horrors of World War I were caused in part by the susceptibility of large populations to manipulation by propaganda. Richards's work inspired the belief that the kind of reading that, on the one hand, allowed someone to overcome stock responses to a poem would also allow her to read and hear public speech critically. As that movement for critical reading developed in the 1930s, one of the motivations for the practice of American New Criticism was to defend the autonomy of literature against the manipulation of literature—at first by Communist-affiliated writers and critics, but shortly enough by the fascists, as in Kenneth Burke's 1939 essay "The Rhetoric of Hitler's 'Battle.'"[1] In later decades, with regard to the Vietnam War, we continued to have the claim that real analytic close reading would allow you to see through the deception. So, in a way, deconstruction arises in response to the eighteen-minute blank space on the Nixon tapes. That is not quite a full historical view, but it is true that those who practice close analytic literary or humanistic reading have said, for nearly a century, that our work has something to do with the way public discourse works. Of course, these attitudes and insights did not stop World War II or other subsequent conflicts and injustices from happening. Do we still think, as I believe we do, that this is the right thread of argument to make? In our conversation now, is there something that distinguishes ethical reading from its antecedents?

DEREK ATTRIDGE: I don't have an answer, just a thought that is not my own but from the pen of J. M. Coetzee in *Diary of a Bad Year.* The partly autobiographical character JC in that book asks himself how American politicians can use language in such a slippery, devious, and manipulative way, and JC concludes that it is perhaps because they were trained in the classrooms of deconstructionists and poststructuralists in the 1960s and 1970s who taught that language is slippery and that there's no such thing as true meaning. I am not sure that either Coetzee or I buy that argument, but it is a different view. In asking now what an ethics of reading might be, it may be that we are thinking more rigorously about the political consequences of how we understand language and interpretation.

QUESTION FROM AUDIENCE: I want to suggest that we flip the terms, and instead of asking about the ethics of reading perhaps we should be asking about the readability of ethics. In looking at the question solely from this perspective of literary analysis, we are overlooking recent philosophers who, in order to do ethics, have turned precisely to literature. I am thinking of Stanley Cavell, Richard Rorty, Martha Nussbaum, and Robert Pippin, among others.

It seems to me that the point about reading is that ethics itself requires all the things we are associating with reading. So it is not as if we are importing ethics to reading all of a sudden to save the discipline or our relevancy, but in fact we are trying to make a point about how we should be doing ethics, and not necessarily about how we should be doing reading.

WILLIAM GERMANO: At Cooper Union, our students will take maybe one or two electives while studying, say, mechanical engineering or architecture, so that really ups the ante on how you are going to do your humanistic pedagogy. In this context, where literature is not your major and you only have exposure to one or two courses, I read literature with my students because these books present problems for analysis. *Othello* presents problems. I know it is corny, but I say to the students coming in that they will take courses in the humanities where we will not solve the problems posed, but we will learn how to think about them, and that I think the tools of learning how to think about problems posed in a text will stay with the students all their lives.

KIM LANE SCHEPPELE: I wanted to comment on this question of whether the problem of the Torture Memos was in the writing, reading, or doing. As Patricia Williams said in her essay, the legal framing of something has consequences. As soon as something is labeled as legal, as law, then the doing of it flows from that labeling.

Here are some sentences from one of the Torture Memos produced under the Bush administration. This memo specified what interrogators could do to Abu Zubaydah, a Saudi Arabian prisoner being held by the United States under suspicion of his connection with al Qaeda. The memo authorizes waterboarding, but also responds to a particular question posed by the interrogators who had learned that Abu Zubaydah was afraid of insects. The Department of Justice is asked for its legal opinion on whether the interrogators can put the prisoner in a box with insects. Here is what the lawyers say:

> As we understand it, you plan to inform Zubaydah that you are going to place a stinging insect into the box, but you will actually place a harmless insect in the box, such as a caterpillar. If you do so, to ensure you are outside the predicate act requirement, you must inform him that the insects will not have a sting that would produce death or severe pain. If, however, you were to place the insect in the box without informing him that you are doing so, then, in order to not commit a predicate act, you should not affirmatively lead him to believe that any insect is present which has a sting that could produce severe pain or suffering or even cause his death.

Then there is a redacted section, and the memo continues:

> So long as you take either of the approaches we have described, the insect's placement in the box would not constitute a threat of severe pain or suffering to a reasonable person in his position.[2]

I want to say a couple of things about this. First, it is the specificity of the language here that produces its effect. The specificity of the language makes people believe the action is legal and that some lawyer thought about it, and it also eliminates the horror of the doing because you go through it first in the writing/reading. Second, anyone who can remember

Winston and Room 101 and the rats of George Orwell's *1984* would be able
to understand what is wrong with this because the scenario is almost
exactly the same. You wonder how anyone could have seen this memo
and not think of *1984* once the interrogators in that book discovered
that Winston Smith was afraid of rats. The failure to make that connection with one of the signature horrors in our recent literature is itself
horrifying.

MR: Would if be more or less horrifying if you learned that the authors of
the memo had been taught *1984*? If they were better readers, would they
be more or less likely to be torturers? I suppose I am expressing a lack of
confidence that teaching reading would actually reduce torture.

III

The Humanities and Human Rights

The Call of Another's Words

Jonathan Lear

It at least seems possible that we can look on others from a third-person perspective and conclude that their conditions of living—their level of poverty, malnutrition, or sanitation, their being subjected to torture or slavery—are such that their basic dignity as a human being is being violated. The thought seems to be available that they have a right to better treatment. Here the methods of measurement perfected in the social sciences can play an invaluable role, both in giving us an accurate sense of what these conditions of deprivation consist in and by helping us to see what forms of response make a measurable difference. We may thereby be able to formulate an adequate social policy.

But this kind of response depends on an agreed upon understanding of what a human rights violation is, and that gives rise to three problems. What if there is little agreement about what human dignity consists in? Or what if there is agreement, but that agreement is significantly mistaken? Or what if there is agreement and the agreement focuses on a worthy goal, but there is nevertheless a disconnect between what people take themselves to be agreeing on and how they actually live their lives? It seems to me that in each of these cases, an engagement with the humanities can make a difference. I want to say a few words about what kind of difference this might be, and I want to focus on the third possibility, in which a gap has opened up between how we view ourselves as living and how we are living. This is a peculiar form of insensitivity, one in which our very awareness of and objection to an injustice can help to sustain the injustice.

In the tradition of the humanities, I would like to tell you a particular story. In the fall of 1987, Peter Brooks was director of the Whitney Humanities Center at Yale and I was a fellow there. There were regular Friday lunches in which fellows would present works in progress, and one week William Cronon gave a talk about how to write a history of the West, one in which the land and environment would foreground the narrative, with the travails of humans in the background. In passing he quoted Chief Plenty Coups, the last great chief of the Crow tribe, on life after the move onto the reservation: "After the buffalo went away, the hearts of my people fell to the ground and we could not lift them up again. After this, nothing happened." I was struck by the power of those words, but that was it. The lunch ended after a discussion.

About fifteen years later, I was taking a familiar walk along Lake Michigan, letting my mind wander, and those words of Plenty Coups came back to me. It was a startling experience because I was not particularly thinking of anything. But it was not just that these words came from out of the blue. There was something special about the manner of their presentation: as though some kind of response was called for. I had no idea what that response might be—that was enigmatic—but I did have a sense that these words had found a target, and in this case the target was me. This vulnerability to being struck by the words of another is, I think, a moment of aesthetic receptivity, and it at least has the potential for disrupting us out of familiar routines.

I bought Plenty Coups's biography and discovered that these words only came in an appendix. The book is in the "as-told-to" genre. The author, Frank Linderman, a white man who lived in Montana as a hunter and trapper, had become Plenty Coups's friend.[1] The book is taken up with Plenty Coups's stories of growing up in the traditional ways, battles against the Sioux, and hunting and nomadic life. But in the appendix, Linderman says that he could not get Plenty Coups to talk about life after the Crow moved onto the reservation. It is only when repeatedly pressed that Plenty Coups uttered those haunting words. As a psychoanalyst, I am fascinated by speech that does not want to be spoken. But I am not here interested in analyzing Plenty Coups's reluctance; rather, I am trying to

describe a process of crystallization that occurred in me. I had no particular interest in writing a book about Plenty Coups, but I did want to respond to him somehow.

This is how my book *Radical Hope: Ethics in the Face of Cultural Devastation* was born.[2] I mostly want to tell you about what happened after the
book was published, but there is something about the peculiarly humanistic engagement with Plenty Coups's words that made the aftermath possible. If I were in the social sciences, I would be under pressure to determine
what actually happened, to record, analyze, and transmit the available data.
But I wanted to write an essay on what Plenty Coups *might* have meant
by his words. Might he have been standing witness to the collapse of temporality? And, if so, what would that witnessing consist of? In effect, I
wanted to make an imaginative possibility robust. This does not mean
one can just make things up. I wanted my investigation of Plenty Coups
to be constrained by all known facts about him, about Crow life, about
the life of the Plains Indians, and about the history of the West in that
period. So I immersed myself for several years in Native American studies
and histories of the West; I made visits up to the Crow reservation and
talked to whomever would talk to me; I hiked through the land Plenty
Coups described, into the Crazy Mountains where he had his vision, and
went to the sites of his battles. Yet I never thought of myself as getting
beyond what he might have meant. (And, of course, as Kierkegaard taught
us, with a knight of faith or a knight of infinite resignation we could never
know on the basis of empirically available evidence whether we were
in the presence of one.) The important point is this: If one can succeed in
making an imaginative possibility robust, it can have a profound effect on
how we live our lives. For our lives are shaped not just by what we take to be
the case, but also by our sense of what is possible. Once an imaginative possibility is opened up, there is room for it to become a practical necessity.

After *Radical Hope* was published—and this must be *the* postmodern
event in my life—I was invited up to the Crow reservation to discuss it.
The Crow themselves were reading the book and wanted to talk about it.
I was to address the assembled faculty, deans, and students of Little Big
Horn College. That I came from a humanities background was crucial to
making this occasion a success. I told them, first, that I was no expert on
Plenty Coups and could do no more than share with them a sense of what
he might have meant and why that might matter, not just to the Crow but
to all of us. Second, I said that I was not there in any way to study them.
You will not be surprised to learn that the Crow are both weary and wary
of being studied.

The conversation that began that day continues. A number of tribal elders invited me to come back and keep talking with them. So I have been going back about four times a year, and we spend the day around a seminar table or hiking into the mountains, talking about the problems they face. My Crow friends also visit me in Chicago. One of my Crow friends had a dream in which our discussion group was given a name, Medicine Dream, so we are Medicine Dream. And we became a "we" in conversations that began in, and have been sustained by, our shared responses to Plenty Coups's words. Two of the members have adopted me into their family as their brother, so I now have an extended family among the Crow. We talk, for instance, about the meaning of water: how water is sacred to them, how the natural springs are threatened by mining projects, how difficult it is to pass on the sacred meaning of water to the younger generation. One August, my family and I lived up in the Wolf Mountains, and my Crow friends would stop by unannounced for a meal and a chat.

In the course of these conversations and developing relationships, my understanding of the wrong the Crow have suffered has shifted. So has my sense of how I am implicated. When I began my work, I thought that the Crow had faced a catastrophic trauma and were now living in its historical aftermath. I now think the trauma persists in the present. Consider, for example, the question "What does it any longer mean to be Crow?" Even from the perspective of a sympathetic outsider, it is so easy to hear this question in the register of the superego. We hear it as asking how the Crow in the present reservation period could possibly live up to the traditional ideals of being Crow. It sounds like a problem of belatedness. But in conversation with my Crow friends, I have come to hear the question differently. The question is at the very center of their lives, and it is not being asked in a superego voice. Rather, it is in the register of irony—an utterly earnest irony about how to be. It expresses a fundamental anxiety that marks their lives. Theirs is not a concern that they fall short of a now impossible ideal; it is a concern that there is no longer an ideal to fall short of. And it is not at all a concern about being too late; it rather expresses confusion about what it means to be in the present. The psychoanalytic model of intergenerational transmission of trauma is appropriate. Six generations after the catastrophe, the trauma is still alive in the present, inflicting psychic and cultural harm on present generations.

I do not know how I could have come to see this without the interpretive approaches that are a hallmark of the humanities and the human relations that have grown out of shared interpretive responses. Obviously, when the formal and final causes of a culture are destroyed—and I do think one needs these Aristotelian categories to understand what happened—one should not be surprised that there are myriad manifestations that can be measured: for instance, poverty, failure to thrive in educational institutions, alcoholism, and methamphetamine addiction. This can encourage the illusion that, in this catalogue of deprivations and harms, nothing is missing. But what is missing from the list is that condition in virtue of which these measurable harms are showing up. This is the destruction of the formal and final cause of Crow life. It is both crucial and incredibly tricky to capture this harm—the one that can never show up on a list of measurable harms but is somehow explanatory of the fact that there is such a list. ·

It is crucial because unless one can somehow grasp the loss, there is no way to mourn it, nor is there a way to craft an appropriate response. One can keep trying to address manifestations of the loss—for example, trying to improve reading skills in school—but the loss itself persists. And it is tricky because although there has been a trauma to the culture, there is no one-to-one relation between that trauma and any psychological trauma to the individual bearers of the culture. One cannot make direct inferences about the psychological states of the individuals. Bearers of a culture may react in all sorts of ways to a traumatic blow to their culture: Some may abandon the culture and try to adopt the dominant one; others may insist on the traditional ways in spite of the fact that they have become impossible; others may have large families, while others give up on family; some may get depressed, some anxious, and some may try to act as though nothing has happened.

Yet the loss must necessarily show up *somehow* psychologically. This is because a form of life is significantly constituted by the actions of the participants, and these actions are necessarily psychologically represented. This is one exemplification of the basic truth that, in general, people can say what they are doing. So if there is a breakdown in the doings of the culture, there must correlatively be a breakdown in the practical understanding of the participants. At this level, it is the language of practical reason, rather than psychological diagnosis, that seems most applicable. If there is a destruction of the formal and final cause of a culture, there must necessarily be a breakdown in the practical self-understanding of the participants.

In a funny way, I have been slowly working my way backward through Plenty Coups's utterance. *Radical Hope* was about Plenty Coups's claim, "After this, nothing happened," but now with my Crow friends I am focused on "the hearts of my people fell to the ground *and they could not lift them up again.*" This is not just metaphor, and it is not simply a psychological description of personal heartache; it is an attempt to communicate a practical harm that has befallen them: the inability to lift their hearts up again. This is, as I now understand it, an inability to commit to a formal and final cause because there is none that presents itself as a heart-lifting option.

I do not know whether this story has a beginning, a middle, and an end. But I shall conclude with a vignette. At the end of *Radical Hope*, I talk about the need for a new generation of Crow poets. These words resonated with a young Crow poet and fiction writer, who ended up applying and being admitted to the Committee on Social Thought at the University of Chicago. He has been studying with us for the past few years and, indeed, will begin his Fundamentals Examination shortly. Scott is the grown son of one of the members of Medicine Dream, and he has himself become a member. He is now a resident head of one of our undergraduate colleges. He and Mark Payne, a classicist who is also a colleague in the Committee and someone deeply interested in Native American affairs, and I have become a Chicago-offshoot of Medicine Dream. Mark is an amazing linguist, and he and Scott are learning Crow on the University of Chicago campus. Together with our Crow friends and family on the reservation, we have unearthed over a thousand pages of unpublished manuscripts from the basements of the Field Museum in Chicago and the Museum of the American Indian in Washington. They were written by curators and anthropologists who visited the Crow at the beginning of the reservation period. Their aim was to purchase artifacts for collections, but they used the occasion to record extensive oral histories about contemporary life on the reservation, memories of the pre-reservation period, and accounts of the Crow approach to the sacred. The three of us have been meeting weekly these past two years to read through these manuscripts line by line, as one might interpret an ancient text. Scott is able to read about his own ancestors and the ancestors of his friends in these unpublished texts, and he can think about these century-old efforts of members of the dominant culture to come to grips with the transformation in the lives of his own people. We are bringing this all back to Medicine Dream for further discussions on the reservation. This is a collaborative effort in which the Crow are coming to say for themselves what this means. Where all this is ultimately going I cannot say. Perhaps it will peter out, or perhaps Scott will find other things to do that have nothing to do with being Crow or being an Indian. I hope he finds ways to flourish, and I have no particular views about what they should be.

But I have become convinced that *if* there is someday to be an appropriate response to the harms inflicted upon the Crow by the dominant culture, it will not just be in the dimension of righting measurable wrongs, but in a *poetic* response that not only reinvigorates Crow imagination but also manages to strike a chord in the souls of we members of the dominant culture. We all know that American history is stained by the appalling treatment of indigenous peoples, but there is a serious question as to how much the familiarity of that knowledge induces its own lethargy. Certainly, I can say in my own case, before I was snared by Plenty Coups's words, I thought I understood at least some of the history and plight of Native Americans. I now think that that purported understanding functioned in me as the basis for a complacency I did not recognize as such. We need the poetic words of another to *wake us up*. Obviously, it is not easy to say what this consists of. We are all familiar with examples of advocacy fiction that leave us cold. Still, we also know that there can be occasions in which we are struck, confronted, and implicated by the words of another in ways that both draw us out of ourselves and toward our own humanity and the humanity of others. This seems to me one way in which the distinctive voice of the humanities can play a crucial role in helping us come to appreciate basic violations of human rights.

On Humanities and Human Rights

Paul W. Kahn

Teaching in a law school, I am surrounded by colleagues who understand themselves to be social scientists. They pursue inquiries in economics, psychology, history, and regulatory administration. Their work usually begins with collecting data in forms that can be measured, and they use that data to formulate testable hypotheses. The ambition of their work is to propose legal reforms. A typical human rights inquiry for these social scientists of the law would be to gather data on whether there is any relationship between signing a treaty and State behavior. The reform ambition would be to tell us what should be done, if there is no such relationship, or how to strengthen it, if there is. Of course, I am not the only humanist working in the building, but all of us suffer from the sense that we are only ornamental: We are tolerated in order to make the school more attractive to the rest of the university.

My colleagues frequently ask me, "What is the evidence to support your claims about the nature of law or the legal imagination?" They expect me to cite polling data or perhaps to design social psychology experiments. How else can we "know" what people think? I respond that there is no reason to prefer a poll to a film, and that we learn what people think by looking at the products of their imaginations—books, poetry, films, political rhetoric, judicial opinions, performances, and practices. The evidence for my claims, I argue, is all around them. To understand it, however, one has to give up measurement and take up interpretation.

Often, I work through a sustained engagement with a text: for example, *Marbury v. Madison*, *King Lear*, *Genesis*, or Carl Schmitt's *Political Theology*. My social scientist friends cannot understand why this could be a useful way to go about studying modern law or politics. They are even more puzzled when I tell them I am not trying to discover what it was that the authors of these texts thought. In my book on political theology, I put it this way: I am not trying to think about, but rather to think with, Schmitt. When I claim not to care what Schmitt thought, my colleagues do not see how my work is an interpretation at all. They think that without such an object of inquiry—something objective—there is no way to measure the truth of a proposition. About this they are right: Truth is not something measurable that stands apart from the interpretation any more than beauty stands apart from a work of art. One interpretation can only be met by another interpretation.

What I have called "thinking with" is what the humanities have always taught. It is a kind of conversation, the aim of which is not to discover authorial intent but rather to create something new: an interpretation. If there is anything exceptional in my work, it is only in the place from which I work and the subjects I take up. I have explored that set of beliefs, practices, expectations, and habits of mind that create and sustain the horizon of understanding—the social imaginary—within which law works. I have been less concerned with the content of legal rules than with the world of meaning within which those rules operate. These inquiries have led me to emphasize aspects of political experience that do not appear to the social scientist—for example, sovereignty and sacrifice, as well as love and faith. To my colleagues, this approach makes little sense.

The dispute here goes to the very heart of the disciplinary divide between the social sciences and the humanities. A lot is at stake in this divide—not just what we ask and how we answer, but what we learn of ourselves when we reflect on the process of inquiry. It is this second point that I want to focus on in the rest of this essay, for thinking about humanistic inquiry may help us to begin to fill the empty space at the foundation of human rights law.

There is an idea of the relationship between human rights and the humanities that goes something like this: Reading a novel or watching a film creates a sympathetic connection to those who are different from

ourselves. We see people who are not members of our families or communities, political, ethnic, or religious. We learn that we share the same
ambitions, concerns, and values. They too have children, parents, and
friends; they too struggle with power and subordination. Their triumphs
and defeats are like our own. Most of all, we learn that their pain is like
our own. Pain is a universal currency that cuts across all other sources of
division: We suffer pain as individuals. Confronting the other's pain in
these imaginative works, we learn that all people deserve our sympathy,
and out of that sympathy comes respect for their human rights.

Sometimes, this claim is packaged within a historical narrative that
looks to new forms of aesthetic production in the modern era. Efforts are
made to trace human rights law to an eighteenth-century sensibility cultivated by new works of imaginative production. A global legal order expresses the juridification of a morality that was already operating in these
creative works.

I do not think there is much to this view, at least in its historicized
form. It borrows too much from the conventional story of civilization's
progress. It drafts Facebook into the same enterprise as Rousseau. More
importantly, we did not have to wait for the modern novel to confront the
message of universal sympathy. This idea is as old as the West. It is already present in the book of Genesis. It is the message of Christianity. It
was there when Las Casas debated Sepúlveda on the recognition of Native
Americans.

The problem is that this idea of universal sympathy has never been
the only value put forward. Our moral history is complicated because our
values and beliefs are not well ordered under a single guiding principle of
universal recognition. Christianity was not just a narrative of love, but
also of sacrifice. We simply cannot say whether the religion of universal
love brought us more peace than war. Nineteenth-century sensibilities in
the United States, even among university graduates, led us to pursue ideas
of manifest destiny at home and empire abroad. Europeans of the early
twentieth century were not differently situated with respect to these values, yet they willingly gave up two generations of young men to slaughter.
The graduates of our humanities programs have never had any trouble
entering into positions of responsibility and power in a society divided
along lines of class, gender, and wealth. Training in the humanities long
seemed compatible with support for both Jim Crow laws and a subordi-
nated working class. More recently, our humanities graduates have had
no trouble taking up careers in global finance. They may defend human
rights even as they benefit from the gross inequalities that perpetuate the

conditions that lead to violations of those rights. What exactly did they learn from us?

The problem is not that the study of texts in the humanities ignores values of recognition and dignity. Rather, there is no single message in these texts. Great works are, almost by definition, morally complex. At the center of the Western imagination is not just the peaceable kingdom of love, but the act of sacrifice for the sake of love. Inclusion is never without boundaries, and thus it is unavoidably tied to exclusion. Violence is as much an act of meaning creation as lawmaking is. Contemporary aesthetic productions frequently take up the question of what we will give for love. When we read violence as sacrifice, we begin to approach the complex character of the modern, political imaginary.

The American legal imagination, like many of our works of aesthetic creation, occupies a space of reason and love, of law and violence. This is a field of political practice in which sacrifice is always a possibility. Our basic narrative offers us law—the Constitution—as the product of an originary act of sacrificial violence by the popular sovereign—revolution. This structure is re-created whenever we imagine an act of sacrifice for law.

The humanities can and should explore the complex ways in which law gains meaning from representation of our collective identity. There is no way to carry out this inquiry except by interpreting the works of the imagination. We should not, however, assume that such an inquiry will make us or our students advocates of human rights law. Indeed, I think the opposite may be more likely: We will come to understand better why human rights law has so little traction as law in the United States. Exploring the relationship between popular sovereignty and law, we will understand better why, for many if not most citizens, international law, including human rights law, does not appear to be law at all. In simplest terms, Americans are not prepared to sacrifice for this law. A law that cannot support sacrifice is one that lacks a connection to the popular sovereign, and that seems not to be law at all. From this comes much of American exceptionalism, including our preference for civil rights over human rights. We can put the same point another way: Human rights law envisions a world without violence, but in such a world there is no place for sacrifice. Whatever we might think of that as a political ideal, the humanities are not about to move us away from the sacrificial imagination.

I am, then, a skeptic with respect to any claim that the study of the humanities will lead us from exceptionalism to universalism, from sacrifice to contract. That, however, is not the end of the story. For unlike the social sciences, the humanities invite us to take up an attitude of self-reflection. What does the act of interpreting tell us about ourselves? While the humanities cannot easily turn us from civil rights to human rights, perhaps they can offer us a way to think about the foundation for a belief in human rights.

Human rights law has long been haunted by the fear that in the absence of a common faith, the project lacks a foundation adequate to the claims of the skeptic. Practitioners tend to rely on positive law, but that will not do much work against the State that rejects a treaty—the United States has rejected many. Apologists claim that human rights emerged from a collaboration among individuals representing all of the major faiths. That is doubtful on its face, but hardly an answer to those who claim no religion but politics or who read their faith differently. I suggested above that efforts to ground human rights law in sympathy for the pain of others cannot work so long as the political imagination values sacrifice. What is left?

Working in the humanities, one always labors in the face of a mystery: There is a gap between what we know and what we create. There is no formula to be followed in painting a picture or writing a novel. There are no rules to be applied. Creation is not production. This leads to a particular existential anxiety. Because the artist cannot explain how she produced her past work, she can never know whether she can do it again. She looks at her own work with the same wonder that you or I might, for she cannot claim possession of it. Rather, she is more likely to say that the work claimed her. We speak of writer's block, but the same experience is true in all the arts.

This sense of the wonder at creation is characteristic of work in the humanities. This, I think, is what we are really trying to teach our students: a sort of humility before the power of creation that is revealed through the subject, but is not possessed by the subject. We teach them this by asking them directly to take up the task of creation, for the process of interpretation is no less a creative act than that of aesthetic production. Every creative work is an interpretation, and every interpretation is a creation.

Asked to interpret some work, I do not know what I will say until I say it. I cannot apply a rule; I cannot simply make the work speak in its own voice. Instead, I engage in a kind of conversation. I think with it. As in any conversation, I hold open the future and expose myself to a sort of risk. The largest risk is silence; the wonder is that something that had been unimaginable before comes into existence. The humanities, in other words, do not just take up creative work as their object of study; they are in themselves a process of creation.

This is why we often structure our pedagogy around asking students to compare two works: The assignment asks the students to create something new. Putting the texts in a common space is an act of creation, and the student must say something new. He cannot look up the answer and cannot simply repeat what the texts say. There is nothing there to be discovered; rather, a common world is to be made. The student must make the works speak to her, but can only do so by speaking to them.

Our experience of ourselves as free is this experience of creating a common world. Once we begin creating/speaking, there is simply no end to it. Every text creates the possibility of such an endless conversation. We do not ask of that conversation whether it is making progress; rather, we ask if it is still interesting. The conversation never ends of its own, but rather it ends because we cannot physically sustain it. We learn then of the weight of the body on the soul—that is, we experience from within another version of the gap between our finite and our free selves.

Creation and interpretation are both free acts. They are not free in the sense of without constraint, but free in the sense of without causal explanation. They are, therefore, beyond the reach of the social scientist. The social scientist's demand for the facts separates him from the world that he studies. The humanities are in the business of transgressing this line of separation, which is only another way of saying that the truth of an interpretation is not separate from the act of interpretation. This is what I meant when I said that one interpretation can only be met by another interpretation.

This experience of free creativity, which goes to the heart of who we are but remains a mystery, is as close to the sacred as many of us are likely to get. It was once explained by speaking of the muses, or inspiration, or grace. When we look at any great work, we simply cannot imagine how the artist did this. Or rather, we can imagine it but cannot explain it. We can imagine it because in our own way we are constantly discovering our own freedom. Shakespeare is a mystery, but so then is my writing of this little essay. I do not know now how I will answer the questions to come, but I act with the faith that our engagement will bring something new into the world. Indeed, it will re-create the world, for every conversation offers a new starting point from which to see the whole. Implicit in this faith is the belief that every person stands within this same mystery of creation, and this is worthy of our respect.

If we take this to heart, if we teach this to our students, we may arrive at the foundation of a belief in universal dignity. Here, we can begin to locate an idea of dignity that does not rely upon sympathy for the suffering body. In place of the body in pain, we find an experience of self-transcendence. To link dignity to freedom and freedom to creation is to recover the link of human rights to revolution. We might, however, think of this as the humanities' reading of revolution, which does not wait for the extraordinary political event, but reminds us that the same free imagination is at work in every discursive exchange. The humanities are not likely to change our political beliefs and practices, but thinking within the humanities may still tell us something about why every person deserves our respect.

Responses and Discussion

Kim Lane Scheppele

HUMANISTIC TACTICS: HUMAN RIGHTS AND THE HUMANITIES

Jonathan Lear alerts us to the importance of listening to others, sitting with others, and reading together—the interpretive moments of humanistic activity. He calls our attention to recognition, dignity, and human rights. Paul Kahn reminds us of the way that law as an interpretive and text-based enterprise stands between State power and its effects. He calls our attention to interpretation, evasion, confrontation, and the complexity of tradition and human rights. Fundamentally, I agree with both of their essays. Both give us a window into how the humanities can enlarge our conception of human rights.

Human rights aim at ensuring that all people, taken one by one and in conjunction with each other, have the possibility of self-authorship. For it is not just freedom from torture, or the right to liberty or freedom of speech, or the right to vote that are at stake in ensuring human rights. All of these things aim at ensuring the dignity of individuals, and hence enlarging their capacity and possibility for self-authorship.

To show what I mean by self-authorship, and in the spirit of telling stories (something that can be understood as a humanistic method), I want to
look at the tactics people deploy when their dignity is infringed, when their
human rights are limited. These are examples of the way the humanities
create possibilities for resistance in repressive regimes.

In regimes that infringe on human rights, we can see the centrality of
what I will call humanistic tactics among those who resist. Resisters use
irony, mimesis, and multivalence. They stand in the interpretive space
between the power of the State and its effects. Resisters often comply with
repression but with an asterisk or an ellipsis, a message that reads differently in different interpretive communities. Knowledge of literature—of
strategies of reading, of cultures of interpretation—are crucial to self-
authorship in this context, particularly when other resources are unavailable. In general, but especially in regimes where human rights are scarce
on the ground, humanistic tactics may be the last refuge of dignity.

Let me illustrate with some examples of this kind of resistance during
the Soviet era, because it provides perhaps the clearest case. Serguei Oushakine has pointed out that in the Soviet Union, resisters often engaged in
what he calls "mimetic resistance."[1] In a regime of censorship, precisely
where it was very difficult to criticize the State openly, people quoted the
law of the State back at it. Dissidents would wear signs around their necks
that said "Respect the Constitution," or they would quote article 2 of
the Soviet Constitution: "All power in the USSR belongs to the people."
They would stand on street corners wearing these signs, and the question
became what could the State do? How could it be illegal to quote the language of the State back at it? But because the words were spoken in a different voice, they of course meant something else. A legal system cannot
figure out what to do with this. The law has no sense of irony; the law is
not amused.

In Poland in that era, people put on public dramatic readings of Jaroslav Hašek's novel, *The Good Soldier Švejk*.[2] Written after World War I, the
novel features the hapless Švejk who is, as he frequently reminds readers, a
certified idiot. When the war breaks out, Švejk enlists in the Habsburg
army, proclaiming his loyalty to the empire. But Švejk is, as he told us, a
certified idiot. And so every time he undertakes to be useful, he gums up
the works, he gets in the way of what the army is actually doing, he winds
up being the person who brings the State to its knees. But he does so
while proclaiming his loyalty to State. Had Švejk intended to disable the
Habsburg army, he could not have done a better job. He says one thing

and does another over and over. So, for example, at the beginning of the book when he is rounded up with others at the beginning of the war and put in jail, while others worry out loud, Švejk says,

> "We're all of us in a nasty jam. . . . You're not right when you say that nothing can happen to you or any of us. What have we got the police for except to punish us for talking out of turn?"[3]

When one of his cellmates protests that he is innocent, Švejk responds:

> "Jesus Christ was innocent too . . . and all the same they crucified him. No one anywhere has ever worried about a man being innocent. *Maul halten und weiter dienen* [Grin and bear it, and get on with the job]—as they used to tell us in the army. That's the best and finest thing of all."[4]

In the context of a repressive regime, what would people mean when they quoted this, as the dissidents known as "Švejkologists" did in Poland? In the Hašek novel, you actually never really know whether Švejk is a certifiable idiot or a resister.

In the Czech Republic—Czechoslovakia at the time—there was a feminist rock group named Zuby Nehty, which means "tooth and nail."[5] They were in fact the only women's rock group in Czechoslovakia at the time. They complied with the rules of the State, which required that artists who wrote songs that they wanted to publish or perform to submit their lyrics to the regime for approval. At first Zuby Nehty wrote dark, resisting lyrics, and of course the censors threw them out. The group quickly learned the limitations of the censorship system, and tried something else. They offered a song called "Let Us Rejoice" with the chorus:

> Let us rejoice and let us make merry.
> Let our joy be eternal.
> Let our joy be forever.

The State had no problem with these lyrics, and the song sailed through the censors without trouble. Then, when the song actually appeared, it was set to funereal music, written in a dark and minor key. Censors could do little about it, but it clearly meant—in that context—something other than what it literally said.

In Hungary, István Örkény was famous for his very short, one-minute stories, especially one entitled "Public Opinion Poll." How could you get in trouble for the following?

Public Opinion Poll

What is your opinion of the current system?

A) Good.
B) Bad.
C) Neither good nor bad, but it could be a little better.
D) I want to go to Vienna.

Your philosophical training tends toward?

A) Marxist.
B) Anti-Marxist.
C) Pulp Fiction.
D) Alcoholic.[6]

All Örkény did in the story was pose the questions. Nothing is stated explicitly against the State, and yet . . . .

What you see in these humanistic tactics is the creativity, dignity, humor, and humanity of those who engage with each other in a space that the State seeks to close. In thinking about the conditions of possibility for human rights, we can think about this contribution of the humanities, which is to give us an empowering family of techniques of reading, thinking, working together, building interpretive communities, and understanding that what we say to each other may not have only the meaning that the State can find in those utterances. These are powerful tactics, especially when a State seeks to foreclose the possibility of self-authorship.

Didier Fassin

Five Counterpoints on Humanities and Human Rights

The title of this session is composed of two terms: "humanities" and "human rights." My reading of the two papers presented is that Paul Kahn's provides a suggestive discussion of the first term, *humanities*, whereas Jonathan Lear's opens an illuminating reflection on the second, *human rights*. My brief comment is an endeavor to articulate the two and then engage our conversation a little further.

On the one hand, coming from a distinct intellectual and institutional tradition (the national committee I chaired in France was "for the human and social sciences," and, more generally, the social sciences there have a critical humanities-friendly foundation, where Foucault meets Bourdieu),

I find interesting Paul Kahn's description of what he calls the "disciplinary divide between the social sciences and the humanities," the positivist and formalist perspective of the former versus the interpretive and reflexive approach of the latter. It is ironic, though. Considering the relative marginality characterizing these two academic worlds in the public sphere, one has certainly to interrogate the damaging consequences for both of their mutual ignorance or delegitimization.

On the other hand, whereas human rights discourse is usually about general principles defended in the public sphere (this is what my time as vice president of Doctors without Borders has taught me, and more generally, it is what historians of human rights suggest, from Lynn Hunt to Samuel Moyn), it is remarkable that Jonathan Lear's compelling evocation concerns a personal and intimate encounter with the Crow Indians, initially through a text, later on their reservation, and eventually within archives. But rather than these so-called others, what his search and research mean is what he phrases as "the process of crystallization that occurred in me." This is indeed a stimulating invitation to think about efforts to bring human rights to the world as a move that tells much about "us" and little about "them," when one usually supposes the opposite.

So how can the social sciences contribute to bringing together these two series of issues—the tense links between the humanities and the social sciences, and the ambiguous relationships involved in the provision of human rights? If critique is to be understood, in Judith Butler's terms, as thinking against the obvious, I suggest formulating the critical contribution of the social sciences to the humanities in human rights on five points—or rather, five counterpoints to the obvious.

First, although the two terms are often used interchangeably, including in the presentation of this panel, it may be helpful to differentiate analytically between human rights and humanitarianism. Hannah Arendt's discussion of the end of the former in *Imperialism* and of an embryonic expression of the latter in *On Revolution*, as well as the distinct legal and institutional settings of human rights and humanitarian right, suggest that, whatever overlap there is, human rights are about the defense of dignity while humanitarianism is about the saving of lives. This difference, which traces a fine line between reason and emotion, has political and ethical implications.

Second, whereas the reconstitution of the two parallel moral movements usually goes back far in time to the Enlightenment, the Scottish moral philosophy, the French revolution, the British abolitionist movement, the Greek war of independence, and sometimes even farther, one should certainly think in terms of dual temporality: one of long duration, which provides a genealogy of ideas and sentiments starting in the eighteenth century; and one of short term, which accounts for the increasing invocation of human rights and humanitarianism to justify social, political, military, and of course moral causes and actions during the past two or three decades. This periodization should help apprehend more cogently the recent transformation of the global public sphere and its paradoxical consequences, when wars are qualified as humanitarian and human rights are invoked to stigmatize ethnic minorities or religious groups.

Third, while human rights and humanitarian worlds are often thought as homogeneously grounded on a shared sense of the common good defined by moral philosophers, the sociological study of discourses and institutions reveals disagreements, tensions, and conflicts, whether one considers the qualification of massacres as genocide in Darfur or the violations of rights in the Palestinian territories, the legitimacy of intervening in Libya or the relevance of the media campaign in the United States targeted at Joseph Kony of the Ugandan Lord's Resistance Army. Rather than a consensual realm, the world of human rights and humanitarianism should be regarded as a social field, with harsh competition not only over limited resources from private donations and public aid, but also over the very definition of ends and means.

Fourth, despite the fact that human rights and humanitarianism as we know them have specific origins and are inscribed in a particular narrative, anthropology invites us to acknowledge non-Western traditions, the production of other moral economies and other ethical subjectivities, whether in African, Asian, or Middle Eastern societies. This assertion does not imply, though, that we should reopen the old debate on moral relativism and its declination in terms of clash of civilizations. Rather, it concerns the mere recognition of the intellectual and political problems posed by a representation of the world in which ethics would have only one geography.

Fifth, the imaginary of human rights and humanitarianism is saturated with the generous ambition of the good one can do for others by defending and assisting them. This is understandable and commendable. But we can rethink this moral question in political terms by asking not only what is gained when we use this language, but also what is lost. In particular, it is remarkable that the claim to human rights generally coincides with the decline of social justice in public discourse in the same way as the invocation of humanitarianism frequently corresponds to the disappearing of the voice of those who are only heard via their benevolent spokespersons. These political losses should be a concern, too.

To conclude, critical thinking, which is what we probably all endeavor to achieve, is all the more difficult when the obviousness concerns our very sense of morality and our ethical responsibility to the world—when it challenges Kurtz's vision in Joseph Conrad's *Heart of Darkness* that "by the simple exercise of our will we can exert a power for good practically unbounded."[1] And precisely because of this difficulty, it is all the more necessary.

Discussion Session 3: The Humanities and Human Rights

CHARLES LARMORE: This is a question for Paul Kahn. As you might imagine, my attention was caught by your statement early in your essay that when you are engaged in interpretation you are not concerned with the author's intent. I think that statement stands in considerable tension with your conclusion, where you talked about the productivity and creativity of interpretation, and compared it to a conversation.

What characterizes a good conversation generally, not just with a text? First, let's look at two things emblematic of a bad conversation. One kind of bad conversation occurs when people simply announce back and forth what they already believe. There is nothing productive or creative in this. In another kind of bad conversation, each person spins his or her own wheels, and may in fact be creative and productive with himself or herself, but is not listening to what the other person is saying. Many real conversations fall into one of these categories.

A good conversation, it seems to me, occurs when each person listens and endeavors to hear what the other actually is saying, as opposed to what one expects the person to say. In making that effort, one may be startled into saying things about the subject that one would not have said or thought before. So the productivity of a conversation depends on listening attentively to what the other person is trying to say while doing one's best to grasp the speaker's intention. If that is the mark of a good conversation in general, why wouldn't that be the same in textual interpretation, understood as a conversation?

PAUL KAHN: I don't think we disagree on much here. What do I mean when I say that the point of an interpretation is not simply to articulate the author's intent? I think you just said it as well—the point is mutual reciprocal engagement in which, together, something is created. You have to take the other person seriously, you have to think about what they are saying. But that is not the end point or ambition in itself—that is part of the process of reciprocally interacting. Your two examples of pathological conversation are exactly ones that don't take that reciprocity seriously.

But your model of good conversation does not end or come to rest with one side saying, "Now I understand you." The idea is to create a third, productive element between the two. So the model of interpretation I was offering encourages reciprocal discourse, and that is why I talk about risk and openness, about creating something together. This interaction is not bounded by authorial intent; that is not a limit or truth at which you are trying to get, but an element in the conversation that you are reciprocally having and creating.

EVERETT ZHANG: I have a question for Jonathan Lear. It seems to me that by your work with the Crows you were creating what I would call a kind of postpublication anthropological fieldwork, demonstrating a new form of engagement with the people. You are engaging in a poetic writing that can wake us up and extend the work, but that cannot happen without the anthropological engagement. This is an observation from the perspective of an anthropologist, and I wonder if you had a reflection on that?

JONATHAN LEAR: This brings up the issue of how lines of demarcation are drawn between the humanities and social sciences. What is the line between the two, or how much is that line an ideological construct? This is something that has come up in this symposium, and also for me in the past. I remember when I was at a dinner at Trinity College in Dublin, and a very well-meaning scientist, who was going to be making decisions about the college budget, asked me—and his question was entirely earnest—how can we measure what you are doing in the humanities? What can you show us? It was clear to me then that university budgets were going to be affected by a certain conception of the measurable, and that the issue of whether certain phenomena are measurable has become the place to draw a line. The impact studies and research assessment exercises that have had such a detrimental effect on intellectual life and the humanities in Britain are one manifestation of this. There are debates within anthropology as well as interdisciplinary struggles around these issues.

Now, my work is in an important sense anecdotal. One of the ironies of my engagement with the Crow was that, whatever value there was in this engagement, it would have been much harder if I had come there as an anthropologist. They do not want to be studied. My Crow friends do not want anthropologists there, no matter how much the field has transformed itself over the years. They still see anthropology as a manifestation of the dominant culture's longstanding attempt to subjugate them and other native peoples. How fair or unfair that perception is can be discussed, but I do think that the conversation could not have happened if I had come to the reservation as an anthropologist. I have been adopted into a Crow family, and I had no idea how life-changing that would be for me. It was crucial that I had nothing to measure, nothing to study. I told them that I was there to talk to them about a book I wrote because Plenty Coups's words resonated with me, and if they wanted to keep talking then I would be there to keep talking. I don't know exactly how to theorize or thematize that, but it is a salient cultural fact that I don't think it could have happened any other way.

ERIC GREGORY: I am from religious studies, a discipline where, through critical readings that my students have done in, say, Agamben and Foucault, both human rights and humanitarianism have come to be considered extremely dangerous practices and discourses that further complicity with injustice. Any expression of support for them by me is met with deep skepticism. And I think there is a kind of despair there. I wonder whether, in the humanities, the culture of ideology critique has become so consuming of how we train graduate students and how we talk to each other that any moment of generativity or even poetic response just does not happen. Is there something we can do differently in the way we teach, in the way we read, in the way we are masters of suspicion?

PK: It is interesting to hear that for me because I teach in a law school where students are not at all skeptical in this regard. This is their moment of relief—they want to do the work of human rights and humanitarianism. Some of them have read Agamben and are a little worried, but on the whole this kind of critique is a positive discourse against which they can measure the other things they are doing, like corporate law. So the problem is not framed in the same way. The problem does come in a kind of second order, where they worry about whether some of these interventions—laws and forms of actions—have assumptions about the failure of agency on the part of those for whose benefit they intend to act. But this is a critical self-reflection that should be encouraged in the law school because of the easy assumptions about the positive moral role of intervention in this area. I think we may be on opposite sides of the university, and we should get our students together.

DIDIER FASSIN: Eric, maybe your students are not reading the right Foucault, because much of his later work is very different from the impression that they seem to have. You can tell them that he signed a petition with Doctors without Borders in favor of a humanitarian intervention to save the boat people in the China Sea. I think there is perhaps an oversimplification here of what critique means. For Foucault, reinterpreting Kant's answer to the question "What is enlightenment?," critique means not taking the world as it is for granted. It means to consider that what is could have been different, that it is in part arbitrary, that another state of affairs could have been possible. In the case of humanitarianism, as I have tried to do in my own work, it implies to think of humanitarianism not in normative terms (eulogistic or disparaging) but of historical developments, the signification and consequences of which must be examined.

WILL EVANS: I thought Kim Scheppele made a powerful point that the law constitutively can't recognize irony and irony's power to resist forms of meaning-making that are repressive or tyrannous. That would differentiate it from allegory, for example. I wonder if the panel could address ways in which irony is useful not just for unmaking a community that is not working, but also for reconstituting a community?

JL: I was thinking, in relation to Kim's essay, of an example of Crow humor that goes like this: There is one thing about which the white man has kept his word. They said they were going to put us back on our feet, and they kept their word—they shot all our horses. That is an example of containing a pain in the form of humor and irony, trying to find ways of facing up to and metabolizing loss without sinking into melancholia and depression.

KIM LANE SCHEPPELE: In the Soviet era, irony served to create a community of solidarity against the state. We had Slavoj Žižek here at Princeton recently, and he reminded us of the Soviet era joke in which a guy goes into a café and asks for coffee without cream, to which the server replies, "I can't give you coffee without cream; I can only give you coffee without milk." Those kinds of jokes reflect a shared experience.

What was so interesting and in some ways so tragic about the end of the Soviet world was that suddenly the world was opened up, people could travel, they could read things and say things that they could never read or say before. For some people this was an immense liberation and enlargement of their world, but for others it meant their world fell apart. A great many dissidents, and in particular comedians, had relied on a tight lexical community where irony could be produced because its members could understand that a surface meaning was not the meaning at play. When these worlds fell apart, there was a loss.

Sometimes the ends of repressive regimes are also simultaneously the ends of the resistance regimes that depended on them, and for some people it is difficult to find an alternative world of meaning once that happens. Some of that has to do with the nature of community that irony creates, and what happens when those communities are disrupted by political events.

ELAINE SCARRY: Just a postscript to this conversation: I saw in the paper recently that the Russian police declared it illegal for toys to hold a protest.[1] People were taking tiny little toys and putting them in assembly in a public space holding protest signs. I think this example bears out your point about humanitarian or aesthetic solutions, especially if one thinks of Baudelaire's essay on the philosophy of toys, that toys are our first experience of the aesthetic.[2]

KLS: To bring the regime to arrest toys—which they did in Barnaul, Siberia—is a kind of victory for the protestors. That is how these tactics work.

RICHARD SENNETT: Do you have a feeling now that the resources of the Web and social media are changing the kinds of protests in Eastern Europe, that they are using the kinds of tactics used in the Arab Spring?

KLS: In the work of irony, the Web both helps and doesn't. It opens out the space to give protestors a larger audience and a larger community of support, but it also makes it hard to generate the common interpretive practices that these tactics rely on.

JUDITH BUTLER: I appreciate the discussion of tactics, and I like those tactics, even stand by them, but I am getting nervous about the idea that the humanities can be, or are, valuable as a set of techniques that can be mobilized. I want to suggest that the humanities or reading is not primarily a set of techniques that can be applied. I am always reminding my students of this. There is something about reading in the humanities, or the kind of reading practices that we try to teach or teach about, that is a different kind of practice than the application or use of a technique. Those latter operations would be instrumental understandings of value. I am not trying to be a complete deontologist, and I think I spoke against that in my paper.

In *The Body in Pain*, for example, Elaine Scarry described a certain idea of receptivity that is extremely important to an ethical practice.[3] And Jonathan Lear today talked about being vulnerable to someone else's words years after they were uttered. What is it for those words to affect you and make you inexplicably receptive? I think he said it was aesthetic, and I wonder if we can talk about that aesthetic as having ethical significance without understanding that as a *causal* relationship. That would be a mistaken way to think about this—to imagine that if only we were all good readers we would then be ethical citizens—although there is something about receptivity that can nevertheless make that result possible. Patricia Williams told us about the woman next to her at the airport, and a series of moments where you are not open to what the person next to you is saying, even trying to shut them out—but then something is spoken, and you start to open, and that receptivity emerges into responsiveness, if not responsibility.

I think of *technique* as presupposing a deliberate agent—I use this technique on this text to get at its meaning, or I use this technique on the street to find my way or defend myself. I think we want to avoid seeing the humanities as a set of tools that can be applied. I am concerned about that because it takes the focus away from this other domain in which the aesthetic actually can, on occasion, move us into ethical responsiveness in a different way.

KLS: I agree with what you are saying about technique, but I want to resist your resistance. When techniques of irony emerged, it was not because people had read theory and applied it. Irony became possible because people had constructed communities of meaning that could hide in plain sight. People learned, as a matter of hard practice, that they could say things that were meaningful to each other and yet totally disabling to the state. The state was disabled from intervening in the conversation because what the resisters said had a public meaning that was its first and obvious meaning, but that obvious meaning was not what bound people together. They were bound together by the alternative, ironic meaning. So I am struck by the way these tactics emerged not out of theory applied, but out of a political closure lived. Instead of being simply an application of theories we have, it is a validation, a further refinement, and a testament to the importance of the theory we have.

JB: I am also interested in the sphere of audibility. Under what conditions is the joke heard and registered? How does that work? Or laughter—under what conditions does laughter become subversive or produce new forms of relationships, new modes of valuation?

KLS: Yes, and if the condition of the possibility of that laughter is the repression that made the community possible, how funny is it? It is a fraught form.

Concluding Discussion

The Humanities in the Public Sphere

PETER BROOKS: I thought I might start us off by a remark of Paul Kahn's, or what I thought I heard Paul saying, which is that the truth of interpretation in the humanities is not separable from the *act* of interpretation. I very much agree with this and feel that what we are talking about is an interpretive *practice*, and the people who claim that the humanities speak to the world of value because you become a better person by reading *Clarissa* or *Julie* have got it all wrong. It has nothing to do with the outcome of reading, but the practice of reading.

So I think that when we talk about sympathy or empathy, terms often bandied about, and the experience of the humanities and why it can lead toward an understanding of human rights, we don't mean that in any easy, sentimentalist way, but that the practice of sympathy or empathy through reading should be very much of a discipline, a praxis.

JUDITH BUTLER: Peter, I want to thank you for having brought us together. I think you solicit and facilitate a kind of thinking that helps us all.

I was thinking about that in particular and your relationship with the term *ethics*. You have offered a very strong critique, for instance, of moralism and ideas of narcissistic virtue and I think you have your own skepticism toward certain highly moral ideas of what it is to be a good person as well as forms of moral judgmentalism, and I appreciate that. That opens up the train of thought: What would ethics do that would be something different from hypermoralistic judgment or what Jonathan Lear has called operating in the register of the superego? Can we think an ethics that is not about superegoic condemnation or virtuous self-inflation? I took that as a point of departure in thinking about how best to respond to this invitation, and I think the people gathered here had many really important things to say along those lines.

My sense about human rights is that there is an active debate right now about human rights organizations exercising power to set the agenda for more local struggles and what happens when that occurs. So, for instance, in gay and lesbian human rights debates there is a large question: Do we say, do we give a norm for, what it is to be a rights-bearing sexual citizen, and do we then hold various countries and regions accountable to that norm? Or do we find out a little more about what people actually want in terms of sexual practice, and how they organize locally and through what terms sexual self-understandings are crafted, to see if human rights language or discourse could be more responsive to the language and practice of very specific kinds of movements and struggles? This criticism does not imply that human rights are nothing other than cultural imperialism; rather, it is that the field of human rights has become a place where this debate happens all the time.

For instance, there are human rights organizations in both Israel and Palestine that do the work of measuring. They document how many people living under occupation have been imprisoned and how many people have been in administrative detention without going to trial. We need that kind of measurement, we need those numbers—they are extremely important. At the same time, a lot of people say we can't stay within the human rights framework because the problem is not counting how many violations there are in the so-called Palestinian territories, but asking whether those territories themselves were established through an unjust colonial settlement that needs to be addressed at a more systematic level.

So the critical position is not against human rights as such—everyone relies on those human rights organizations—but asking whether the human rights framework is sufficient for certain kinds of political analysis and political movements organized by the struggle for justice. Human rights are obviously rights-based politics, so we should be asking what rights-based politics allow us to do and what they keep us from doing. A struggle for justice, for freedom—these are large norms, I know. Do I want to become a subject who has these rights such that I can use or exercise them in some way? Or are we actually looking to reconfigure the political field, the political order in a region such that justice and freedom and equality may be better realized? Sometimes rights are a part of that picture, but they are not all of that picture. One might say that there is an insufficiency within the human rights framework without saying that it should be debunked or thrown away, or that it is nothing other than an instrument of cultural imperialism, which I think is rather unthinking.

On another note, I would like to hear more about the practical and about practical reason. I think there is something about the history of practice that is different from technique and also different from the idea of causality. Some of our arguments became problematic when we started asking whether the reading of a text leads to the practice of good deeds. If we construe the relation between text and deed as causal, I think we are in some difficulty because there is always a question of how a text is taken up, or under what conditions it is taken up in one way or another for the purposes of a set of actions or practices.

I also see right now in the academy an effort to rethink critique so that it is not just reduced to suspicion or debunking but so that it becomes a pathway to hope, a way of trying to reconfigure the political field more generally so that we might think differently, of opening up possibilities for living and livability rather than shutting them down.

Lastly, I want to draw attention to humanities in the public sphere by mentioning the book blocs. I don't know how many of you were aware of the demonstrations in Rome and London and various places throughout Europe when this occurred. Students who were protesting massive budget cuts to universities or the closing of public universities took to the streets holding up signs with various titles and authors, effectively saying, "I want to live in a world in which I might go to the university and read such books," and they included Plato, Marx, Althusser, Jane Austen. I think it is important to see that those kinds of public demonstrations are fueled by the desire to read and to secure the institutional conditions for the democratization of reading.

KIM LANE SCHEPPELE: I am going to take up one piece of the challenge to the human rights framework. I share your sense of critique and also your sense that rights should not be thrown out. But one of the worries about the human rights framework is its extreme individualism. Much of the human rights movement was a reaction against the authoritarianism of the twentieth century, and the human rights successes consisted of translating these principles into law. Once you get underneath how those authoritarian systems worked, and in particular how the Soviet system worked, many forms of resistance were collective forms, in which community building and collective solidarity were crucial to how resistance actually happened. Behind the demand for individualistic rights was a collective enterprise of alternative meaning-making.

Those fighting for human rights were not living in an individualized rights-defined space when they made those arguments. Instead, the lives of dissidents represented a meaningful kind of counterpoint to a world of individualized rights. With the end of the Soviet system, we also saw the end of the solidarity of these groups that were resisting power. It's one of the reasons why the creeping authoritarianism we see now in these former Soviet places cannot fully be resisted because the communities that had been formed to resist repression were split up with the "fall of the wall."

So I wonder whether the forms of repression that exist in countries that are allegedly democratic, open, and neoliberal demand a different kind of rhetoric—not the individualism of the human rights framework but something much more solidarity building. Perhaps that is why the Occupy movement doesn't immediately proceed from a rights rhetoric. Often, demands for liberation call for some inverse of what they think they are living through at the moment when they develop the critique. But when the system to which they are objecting disappears and they are left with what they once thought would be better, then they can see that their solutions coexisted with rather than fully opposed the governments they criticized; they were not fully possible under any other.

I am therefore adding the unfolding of time to what you said, Judith.

JONATHAN LEAR: I want to go back to the question about the relationship of the truthfulness of the act of interpretation that Paul Kahn was talking about in his essay. One of the things I am interested in is the fullness of truthfulness. A lot of the work of psychoanalysis is helping or allowing people to speak their minds, where we're not just talking about accuracy of words but about a filling up of being in the verbal expression. Part of the act of creation that Paul was talking about, I think, is the capacity of the humanities to encourage a kind of fullness in truthful speech. And I don't think there is any way to capture that other than as essentially in the first person. It does not have to be first-person singular, it could be first-person plural, but there is no other way to get it.

Judith Butler was raising this question about the practical, and I think that this is also a place where the humanities distinctively can have a role. For instance, when I think back on apartheid in South Africa, there were a lot of things that could not be prevented and a lot of things that humanists could not do, but what stays with me is J. M. Coetzee's *Waiting for the Barbarians*. That, for me, defines what happened there, that is what is lasting: this novelist's attempt to resonate in other peoples' souls as to what this was really about.

DIDIER FASSIN: I have a few points, the first of which gets back to a discussion we had earlier about Agamben and Foucault. It concerns the translation of the humanities and philosophy toward the public sphere in general, and maybe more specifically toward the social sciences. The uses that are made of the humanities often correspond to an impoverished version of philosophical theory. The literal importation of concepts such as biopolitics or bare life, which are applied almost mechanically to interpret the social world, does not account for their complex texture and ends up being antiheuristic. So we need to think about this problem of translation not in terms of dogmatic faithfulness but as *respectful treason*, by which I mean we should translate these theories in a way that keeps them alive and should adopt these concepts only so long as they help us to think further and deeper.

The second point deals with the division between the social sciences and the humanities, which has been described earlier in terms of an opposition between positivism and interpretation. We must be aware that the social sciences are diverse and that they are diversely constituted, depending on national or even local contexts. Anthropology, whether it is qualified as cultural or social, is largely based on an interpretive epistemology. Even sociology, probably much more in Europe than in North America, has an interpretive tradition. But it is correct that certain disciplines, such as economics or politics or international relations, are more inclined to positivism as well as more ready to adopt the language of public authorities and respond to the question "What should we do?," which is not typically the type of question we are very comfortable with. We have to resist this positivist trend, which has gained substantial legitimacy today, being aware that it does not so much separate the social sciences from the humanities but actually distinguishes two ways of thinking about the world, with a line that comes across both domains.

The last point I wanted to evoke concerns human rights and humanitarianism, and our criticism of those whose politics are based on these principles. In fact, social agents, when they use this language to defend their cause, do not necessarily adopt it in an innocent way. They are aware that it is the legitimate language of the moment, which makes it good leverage. Therefore, when we criticize the individualistic approach of human rights or the compassionate move of humanitarianism, we probably neglect the fact that agents involved in these fields are often themselves reflexive about it. When they refer to abuses or exhibit suffering bodies, they use this language as a strategy to claim more broadly social rights or civil rights. They are often less naïve and more "political" than we assume. This is something that ethnography constantly reminds us of: People have a kind of social intelligence.

MICHAEL ROTH: How can we connect what Judith Butler called the desire to read with what Patricia Williams called the renaming capacity, or the ability to notice people, groups, and events and have them count for us? I am thinking of this in a pretty mundane way—that as teachers in the humanities, if we are lucky, we have students who come to our classes with a desire to read. For me, the question is how do we connect that desire to read to this capacity to rename, to remake, to have things count for us, and to a general capacity to not participate in this wave of conformism that is sweeping over the academy? I think the cuts we are seeing in Europe and the United States, and the efforts of administrators to streamline the university under the guise of instrumentality, are creating the university as a site of ultraconformism to current norms.

What we see in our classes—the desire to read, or the desire to be absorbed in a painting, or in a work of music—how can we as professors and teachers turn that into antimoralism and nonconformism, or anticonformism?

BROOKE HOLMES: One thing that hasn't been on the table is the relationship between the humanities and the sciences, to take that extra step as it were. Something that Paul Kahn said really resonated with me in rejecting the idea of quantification. If I understood Paul correctly, there is no causal necessity in the interpretive act, the generative act, the responsive act, so that causal and quantitative analysis will not capture that singularity, that creative energy.

It strikes me that that is an important point to be made not just about the human but also about the nonhuman and the material world more generally right now. We are moving away, and watching the sciences themselves move away, from an understanding of matter in reductive causal terms. So I think there is a moment or a question on the table: Is that causal complexity—the way in which life itself is showing itself to be interpretive, interpreting its surroundings, generative, creative—an entry point for the humanities? If interpretation now is the mark of the humanities, it is also a kind of passageway into thinking about—I do not want to say posthumanities—something that would move us beyond that sphere. So I think there is a kind of invitation to take that point, to think, to go one step farther to the territory of the sciences, where we are in a way least welcome and most afraid of going because for so many years matter was necessity, it was deterministic.

In fact, can we afford not to? Can we afford not to be engaging in those conversations and trying to create hybrid interpretive acts with the sciences or at least to trying to break through that barrier that has been in place, that nature/culture barrier, for so long? We are at a point, I think, historically and theoretically where we might be able to move through it.

PAUL KAHN: I think that's a great point. I completely agree that the next step, the way in which this should be extended, is to be thinking about the relationship between the individual, the State, and the larger universe, cosmos, and nature.

I want to connect this problem of reading and the humanities to an idea of freedom, which I think is the critical idea running through all of this. Jonathan Lear's point, which is why I liked his essay so much, gives us a concrete example—what it looks like in practice, as you were saying. Jonathan, too, made the same point about how it is not causal, and this also goes to your point about the necessity of formal and final causes.

So I think there is a unity of coherent themes here. I do not know if this is right, but I do think there is a bit of inversion. There is this idea now that maybe the humanities were engaged in a critical project and it became seen as kind of destructive or negative—but, of course, negation is also an entry point to creation. Now there is a reconsideration, a reconstruction, so that it is a creative destruction. I think this is also related, Peter, to your point about speaking in different voices, and letting truth be a kind of occupying or taking up of these voices.

JONATHAN LEAR: This has been an intense practical problem for me, as well as for my colleague Mark Payne in his book *The Animal Part*.[1] Instead of the model of the dominant culture teaching the nondominant culture "here are our truths," we need to explore something different. Payne's book looks at the rich history of Latin and Greek poetry that consists of our talking to animals. Part of what makes the book so beautiful, I think, is that rather than a kind of hermeneutics of suspicion in which we assume *a priori* that this did not happen, the *a priori* is "Who knows? Maybe it did." What his book brings to light is a huge, rich Western, Latin, Greek tradition in which we speak to animals and they tell us very important things. And, of course, that is the heart of Crow culture. Two cultures could meet here without one saying, for instance, we cannot learn anything from Western civilization because it is just the white man's corrupt universe, so we have got to go over to the wisdom of the natives, or (on the other hand) we must learn this because it is the wisdom of the West. There is a kind of discovery of a rejected or ignored tradition of talking to animals and them talking to us, and us learning from them. This is one of the places where having this conversation has been a real success.

PATRICIA WILLIAMS: I am actually less optimistic, particularly in the context of bioethics. I acknowledge, as Didier Fassin said, that there are circumstances in which people are using certain vocabulary in very strategic ways. But what really concerns me is the lack of self-consciousness about the way in which certain kinds of determinism are actually being re-inscribed, despite precisely a moment in scientific and technological revolution in which it ought to be exactly the opposite. The human genome project, for example, says that there is virtually no difference among us; yet scientists and science journalists and the media make us think there is a gene for this and a gene for that, even though that is actually not what the data show. It is not a text but a chemical process. For example, I think Skip Gates told the audience on one of his programs that Stephen Colbert was 100 percent white. Now 100 percent white actually refers to the data sets that matched him up with nine people in northern Wales, which was then labeled or called Caucasian (but had nothing to do with the Caucasus) and then that became "white." In expressing it as 100 percent white, it becomes a reinscription of notions of racial purity. That kind of romance really troubles me because a lot of it operates at unconscious levels.

Also, we live in a certain ultralibertarian moment where all our constitutional discourse, all our criminal discourse, and all our tort discourse is ultracontractarian—all in private contract terms rather than social compact terms. That is why I am not sure that even speaking in the first person, alone, is liberating because the first person according to this model is *Homo economicus.*

BH: I think in a way that is precisely why occupying the space where there is neither pure causal necessity nor pure agency is so important. There has to be a space between.

JONATHAN CULLER: The remarks so far have made it clear that there is an endless array of new domains for critical analysis and no end of things for the humanities to address. I have two comments in relation to the previous remarks. First, for a long time, one of the arguments about the value of the humanities was that we did the work of considering what it means to be human. This has often not gained much traction within the university, partly because it is deemed rather abstract and self-serving. But the new domain—the broad domain of human/animal studies—has actually given it a concreteness that makes it available. Also, it does open up possibilities for interaction with scientists, always with a critical edge. So I think the reinvigoration of this discourse about what it means to be human seems to me in some way a more promising domain for the humanities than, say, critical analysis, which has had a good run but may not be doing its work anymore as it used to.

The other thing is that we have been talking a lot about instrumentalization, and I am very aware of this trend at Cornell University at the moment because we are building a campus in New York City that is entirely devoted to technology transfer and instrumentalization. In this domain, some of the scientists—especially, say, the theoretical physicists—are very much on the side of the humanities. They understand better than others in the university that research is about knowledge, and knowledge for its own sake. Sometimes the ideas theoretical physicists come up with may have applications, but many of them do not, and these scientists want to continue their work whether the practical application is evident or not. So they are really very good allies for the humanities, where we also think studying works is a value in and of itself, independent of whether social benefits might accrue.

WILLIAM GERMANO: I want to respond to Michael Roth. We began with Judith Butler's wonderful essay, which hit so many different points that we could spend more time on, but one of them was the notion of metrics.

We are so resistant to metrics. Our conversation today has been very much about the independence of what we do, and the values of freedom that underscore the work of the humanities, yet still I feel we have not articulated anything really to demonstrate the value of what we do. I think, in a curious way, this might be an easier thing to accomplish than to substitute for a metric something else that could satisfy this cultural and social pressure to demonstrate that we at least can prove to ourselves that we accomplish what we say we are going to accomplish.

We are all in institutions where the culture of assessment is absolutely part of the discourse of our departments and programs, yet it is a very awkward conversation to have wherever you go. I do not know whether anybody wants to step into that muddy pool. But I think the notion of having some language that we can use to talk about what *we* see ourselves accomplishing is a crucial piece that is missing in our discourse.

PB: And to the extent that I have looked at the existing models, such as the Collegiate Learning Assessment, they are a total misfit because they are all instrumentalist problem solving, the kind of thing you learn in the first year of Harvard Business School. They have nothing really to do with the kind of practice of reading that we do. I agree with you that we are going to have to come up with some way to self-assess because otherwise someone will impose it.

RALPH HEXTER: I think we are laying out many future conferences with possible connections with the sciences, with bioethics, and with the animal/human. What I was most struck by was when Jonathan Lear described the formal and final causes of a culture being destroyed; given the coming change of our environment, it may be a very powerful opportunity to get a lot more people focused on what we need to be studying and interrogating. At a campus like mine, humanities are a very small part of what we do—we are very much a science campus. So I keep thinking of ways in which the discourses in the humanities can also have resonance among some of the people working in the sciences and other areas, as there is considerable debate going on in those disciplines as well.

ELAINE SCARRY: One postscript—I have no idea whether it is testable that the humanities instill ethical learning, but I remembered that the Hastings Center actually, in the 1980s, did an extensive inquiry into the disciplines and the degree to which they can serve as vehicles of ethical learning.

Literature and history, if I remember correctly, were the two primary disciplines that seemed to be very good, in their view.[2]

Second, I mentioned earlier that I think by not bringing up things like empathy, beauty, and disputation in the classroom we actually diminish the power of these things, and I gave the example earlier of beauty. But I want to talk for a minute about the question of empathy. When we bring up empathy in the classroom, we tend either to celebrate it or disparage it, but not to get beyond that; however, there are very interesting observations that have been made. For example, Walsh McDermott at Cornell Medical often spoke about the fact that whether or not we are good at narrative compassion, when compared with statistical compassion we are brilliant at narrative compassion. That is, we cannot do statistical compassion at all. So I think it is important in class to talk about empathy and talk about the fact that whether we are good at narrative compassion or not, we are dreadful at this other thing called statistical compassion.

Even a novel by Dickens or Zola or Balzac, which may ask us to hold on to the fates of sixty characters, is nothing compared with what we are being asked to think about in political life. We ought to be cognizant of that. On the other hand, I think that literary works are most helpful insofar as they expose the limits of our ability to think empathetically. Novels—and Thomas Hardy is for me an example of this—can show a character to be so substantive and weighty but regarded as weightless by all around her. For instance, by the time Hardy is done describing Tess in *Tess of the d'Urbervilles* (1891), she weighs about a thousand pounds emotionally in our minds, and yet we see the other characters only being able to understand her as a piece of gossip. That is an incredibly helpful model. In literature, the failure to grasp the reality of other people and how they can be injured is often done through underexposure and overexposure, and these are absolutely the ways in which injuries and misrepresentations are carried out in political life and in the media. If all we do in the classroom is say "empathy yes" or "empathy no," we never get to these other important attributes of empathy.

Finally, one last postscript about the idea of critical skepticism. Several people have brought up Geoffrey Harpham's work. His most recent book on the university talks about this dialogue between Michel Foucault (or I think Didier Fassin would say the younger Foucault) and Noam Chomsky.[3] Chomsky allows the words "human nature" to be used but Foucault does not, and a kind of political constraint comes from a prohibition on using that language. One other book that to me has been very helpful is by a young scholar named Christian Thorne, a brilliant investigation of skepticism in earlier centuries and the conservative ends that it serves.[4] He looks at people from Montaigne up through Hobbes, and it is really an extraordinary book because we pride ourselves on thinking that skepticism is going to come out on the side of liberalism—yet that may not be its history at all. It is often very disempowering, making you think it is not actually a tool to be used.

JB: To the question of conformism, we do need ways of evaluating the current metrics, and we need ways of evaluating our own work that rival or contest some of the notions of assessment. I think we need to reanimate critique as precisely a way of thinking about the competing schemes of evaluation and evaluating them.

My last thought is this: There is a little bit of sadness when we talk about metrics or measurement. I think that, although the term connotes the completely quantifiable now, there was a time when we talked about *poetic* measure or metrics, or about measure as an important part of Aristotelian ethics. You know, there is a measure for measure. We have to figure out a measure for measure.

INTRODUCTION

1. The term "Torture Memos" was originally applied to three memos that originated from the United States Department of Justice on August 1, 2002 (and made public later): 1) Memorandum for Jack Rizzo, "Interrogation of al Qaeda Operative"; 2) Memo for Alberto Gonzalez, "Standards of Conduct for Interrogation under U.S.C. 2340-2340A"; 3) Letter to The Honorable Alberto R. Gonzales from John Yoo. Further investigation and attention have brought later documents to light as well. See e.g. David Cole, *The Torture Memos: Rationalizing the Unthinkable* (New York: The New Press, 2009); see also The Torture Archive at http://www.aladino.wrlc.org/gsdl/collect/torture/torture.shtml.

2. Charles J. Sykes, *Profscam: Professors and the Demise of Higher Education* (New York: St. Martin's Press, 1988); Roger Kimball, *Tenured Radicals: How Politics Has Corrupted Our Higher Education* (New York: Harper, 1991); Andrew Hacker and Claudia Dreifus, *Higher Education? How Colleges Are Wasting Our Money and Failing Our Kids—And What We Can Do about It* (New York: Times Books, 2010).

3. Anthony Grafton, "Our Flunking Universities," *New York Review of Books* 68, no. 18 (November 24, 2011), 38–42.

4. Jane Mayer, *The Dark Side: The Inside Story of How the War on Terror Turned into a War on American Ideals* (New York: Doubleday, 2008).

5. Lynn Hunt, *Inventing Human Rights* (New York: W. W. Norton, 2007).

6. U.S. Department of Education, *A Test of Leadership: Charting the Future of U.S. Higher Education*, Final Report of the Secretary's Commission on the Future of Higher Education (2006), www2.ed.gov/about/bdscomm/list/hiedfuture/reports.html.

7. Ibid., 13.

8. Ibid., 4.

9. Richard Arum and Josipa Roksa, *Academically Adrift: Limited Learning on College Campuses* (Chicago: University of Chicago Press, 2011).

10. Wallace Stevens, "Notes toward a Supreme Fiction," in *Collected Poems* (New York: Knopf, 1961), 383.

ORDINARY, INCREDULOUS

1. The National Humanities Alliance, in opposing the cuts to the National Endowment for the Humanities, takes the tack that one needs to restate the obvious: "The public value of the humanities is unquestioned. They enrich individual lives, they bring communities together, they underpin our civic institutions, they bring forth our history and our shared values, they make possible how our heritage is understood and preserved, and they support a broadly educated and competitive workforce." Michael Brintnall, President, National Humanities Alliance, House Congressional Testimony FY 2012 National Endowment for the Humanities, Public Witness Testimony Submitted to the Interior, Environment, and Related Agencies Subcommittee, Committee on Appropriations, U.S. House of Representatives, April 2012, www.nhalliance.org/advocacy/testimony/congressional-testimony-fy-2012-neh.shtml.

2. Lisa Foderaro, "Budget-Cutting Colleges Bid Some Languages Adieu," *New York Times*, December 3, 2010.

3. Scott Jaschik, "Job Freefall, Job Recovery," *Inside Higher Education*, January 3, 2011.

4. Peter Schmidt, "Historians Continue to Face Tough Job Market," *The Chronicle of Higher Education*, January 3, 2011.

5. Christopher Newfield, *Unmaking the Public University* (Cambridge, MA: Harvard University Press, 2008): 208–219.

6. See Michel Feher, "Self-Appreciation; or, the Aspirations of Human Capital," *Public Culture* 21 (2009): 21; Wendy Brown, "Neo-liberalism and the End of Liberal Democracy," *Theory & Event* 7 (2003).

7. See Michelle Ty, "Higher Education on Its Knees," Introduction to the Fall/Winter issue of *Qui Parle* 20, no. 1 (2011): 3–32.

8. In Santorum's words, he was for his instructors "out of the pale"— a fine expression that combines, I surmise, "beyond the pale" with "out of the blue" or "out of the mainstream" and which suggests that he was regarded as outside the realm of the recognizable or that he had descended on that campus from a faraway planet or from the more unsavory recesses of whiteness. I do not think of the Nitney Lions huddled with a strong cohort of Heideggerians as a left-wing outpost, but perhaps that is to mistake the garbled syntax of a fantasy structure for a reasonable report on reality.

9. See Librotraficante.com for information on the Arizona law and its impact.

10. Wendy Brown, "American Nightmare: Neoliberalism, Neoconservatism, and De-Democratization," *Political Theory* 34, no. 6 (2006): 690–714.

11. Louis Althusser, "Ideology and Ideological State Apparatuses," in *Lenin and Philosophy*, trans. Ben Brewster (New York: Monthly Review Press, 1971), 127–93.

12. Ibid., 139.

13. Ibid.

14. Ibid., 171.

15. Ibid.

16. Ibid., 171–172

17. Ibid., 172.

18. Ibid., 173.

19. Franz Kafka, "Description of a Struggle," in *The Complete Stories*, ed. Nahum N. Glatzer, (New York: Schocken Books, 1971), 9–51.

20. Ibid., 35.

21. Ibid.

22. Ibid., 36.

23. Ibid., 34.

24. Ibid., 36.

25. Franz Kafka, *Diaries, 1914–23*, ed. Max Brod, trans. Martin Greenberg (New York: Schocken Books, 1949), 75.

26. Kafka, "Description," 36.

27. Ibid.

28. See Alain Badiou, "Philosophy as Creative Repetition," in *The Symptom* 8 (2009): "Stevens writes: 'We must endure our thoughts all night.' Alas! That is the destiny of philosophers and philosophy. And Stevens continues: 'Until the bright obvious stands motionless in cold.' Yes, we hope, we believe that one day the 'bright obvious' will 'stand motionless.'" I would add the following: For Stevens, it is unclear whether the time when the bright obvious will stand motionless is realizable, although it remains the ideal toward which those who endure their thoughts nevertheless move. If it proves unrealizable, endurance itself is the ultimate.

29. Theodor W. Adorno, "On Lyric Poetry and Society," in *Notes to Literature*, trans. Shierry Weber Nicholsen (New York: Columbia University Press, 1958/1991), 1:43 (italics added).

30. As Randy Martin queries, "How might the humanities turn its own interpretive prowess, which has been developed through a critique of representation in textual forms, to public matters whose value and impact remains still very hard to discern?" in "Taking an Administrative Turn: Derivative Logics for a Recharged Humanities" *Representations* 116 (2011): 170.

31. Geoffrey Harpham, "From Eternity to Here: Shrinkage in American Thinking About Higher Education," *Representations* 116, no. 1 (2011): 57.

32. Wendy Brown, "The End of Educated Democracy," *Representations* 116, no. 1 (2011): 19–41.

33. Dana Villa, *Socratic Citizenship* (Princeton, NJ: Princeton University Press, 2001).

34. See the "Dictionary" subheading at www.Investopedia.com.

35. Ernst Bloch, *The Spirit of Hope*, trans. Neville Plaice et al. (London: Basil Blackwell, 1986).

POETRY, INJURY, AND THE ETHICS OF READING

1. Steven Pinker, *The Better Angels of Our Nature: Why Violence Has Declined* (New York: Viking-Penguin, 2011). I have just summarized Pinker's argument in a much more conservative or modest form than Pinker himself does because I am more certain of its truthfulness in that form. Although his overall argument about the greatly diminished rate of violence does *not* persuade me, certainly his documentation of the many *specific* forms of cruelty that have subsided *does* persuade me. I regard the book as a magnificent achievement on many grounds: the importance of its subject, the ambition of its research and documentation, the eloquent formulation of both historical events and philosophic arguments, and the patience and lucidity of its inquiry. Nevertheless, from my perspective, the book has major substantive misjudgments (most importantly, his belief that use of nuclear weapons is now taboo when in fact it is only public discussion of our ever-ready nuclear arsenal that is taboo) and misleading stylistic habits (such as acknowledging that a given harm occurs at both the outset and the close of a given era—whether millennia, century, or decade—but then using vivid images and numbers only at the terminus that is far away from us and an abstract word at the close-by terminus).

2. Ibid., 173, figure 4–9.

3. Ibid., 173.

4. Ibid., 175, 176, describing Lynn Hunt, *The Invention of Human Rights: A History* (New York: W. W. Norton, 2007), 38–69.

5. Pinker, *Better Angels*, 174.

6. On the difference between legal and literary approaches to injury, see Elaine Scarry, "Das SchwierigeBild der Anderen," in *SchwierigeFremdheit: Über Integration und Ausgrenzung in Einwanderungsländern*, ed. R. Habermas, P. Nanz, and F. Balke (Frankfurt: Fischer Verlag, 1993), 229–264. The English version, "The Difficulty of Imagining Other People," can be found in *Handbook of Interethnic Coexistence*, ed. Eugene Weiner (New York: Abraham Fund, 1998); and in *Human Rights and Historical Contingency*, ed.

Carla Hesse and Robert Post (Berkeley: University of California, 1999). A brief version occurs in *For Love of Country*, ed. Martha Nussbaum and Joshua Cohen (Boston: Beacon Press, 1996).

7. Pope wrote, "Apollo tun'd the Lyre; the Muses round / With voice alternate aid the silver Sound." Ogilby wrote, "Apollo playd, the Muses heavenly Quire / Alternate parts Sung to his Golden Lyre."

8. I am grateful not only to Hobbes (who praises the annotations of Ogilby in the preface to his own translation of the *Iliad*) but to my former research assistant Matthew Spellberg (who located Ogilby's translation in Houghton Library) for bringing me into contact with these rich annotations.

9. See also the translations of Robert Fitzgerald and A. T. Murray.

10. Victor Erlich, "Eclogue," in *Princeton Encyclopedia of Poetry and Poetics*, ed. Alex Preminger et al. (Princeton, NJ: Princeton University Press, 1965, 1990), 212–13. Most strongly associated with Virgil, the eclogue later flourished in the fourteenth through sixteenth centuries.

11. Urban T. Holmes, "Poetic Contests," in *Princeton Encyclopedia*, 626–27. Holmes's article names the multiple forms of debate poetry I cite here.

12. Holmes on "Poetic Contests" and Frank Chambers on "Partimen," in *Princeton Encyclopedia*, 626–27, 603, respectively.

13. Dante Alighieri, *Vita Nuova*, trans. and ed. Mark Musa (Oxford: Oxford University Press, 1992), 86n7.

14. Lawrence J. Zillman, "Sonnet" and "Volta," in *Princeton Encyclopedia*, 781–84, 894, respectively.

15. Holmes on "Poetic Contests," Anna Balakian on "Lauda," Chambers on "Pastourelle," in *Princeton Encyclopedia*, 626–27, 445, 606, respectively. The lauda and pastourelle both begin in the thirteenth century.

16. John Edwin Wells, *A Manual of the Writings in Middle English 1050–1400* (New Haven, CT: Yale University Press, 1916), 411–12.

17. Jean Bottéro, "La 'Tenson' et La Réflexion sur Les Choses en Mésopotamie," in *Dispute Poems and Dialogues in the Ancient and Mediaeval Near East: Form and Types of Literary Debates in Semitic and Related Literature*, ed. G. J. Reinink and H. L. J. Vanstiphout (Leuven: Department Orientalistiek, UitgeverijPeeters, 1991), 15.

18. Herman L. J. Vanstiphout, "Lore, Learning and Levity in the Sumerian Disputations: A Matter of Form, or Substance?," in *Dispute Poems*, 22–23. The cadences of dispute often sound echoic of those we know from Western poetry. In the *Iliad*, Agamemnon says to Achilles in Robert Fagles translation: "Desert, by all means—if the spirit drives you home! / I will never beg you to stay, not on my account / . . . What if you are a great

soldier? That's just a gift of god. / Go home with your ships and comrades, lord it over your Myrmidons! You are nothing to me—you and your over-weening anger!" (Book I, 204–13). So in "Plough vs. Hoe," the Hoe says: "Plough, you may trace furrows— / what is your furrowing to me? / Plough, you may cut furrows— / what is your cutting to me?"

19. Vanstiphout, "Lore, Learning," 25.

20. Thomas L. Reed Jr., *Middle English Debate Poetry and the Aesthetics of Irresolution* (Columbia, MO: University of Missouri Press, 1990), 144–48, 327–28. Even in disputes between the Body and the Soul, the Body gives a strong self-defense. "Joining in the flyting and . . . reviling the Soul for its moral irresponsibility" (157).

21. Reed, *Middle English Debate Poetry*, 103–104. Another reminder that dispute is not limited to the West is the Japanese novel *The Tale of Genji*, written at the time of *Beowulf*. It is laden with poetry contests, drawing contests, and perfume-making contests in addition to disputes between characters.

22. Reed, *Middle English Debate Poetry*, 392, 394, 398, 401, 408.

23. Ibid., 186.

24. Ibid., 43–65.

25. Ibid., 69–70.

26. Ibid., 88–96.

27. Is it the case that dispute poems precede and help to bring into being these three arenas (as literacy, book publishing, and the novel precede the Humanitarian Revolution)? Reed's book is more interested in showing how the university, the law courts, and the parliaments helped to shape poetry—the roll call vote in Westminster imported into Chaucer's *Parlement of Foules* (and see 59, 63, 65, 67, 75, 85, 87–89)—than in showing how poetry shaped these institutions, as when a fourteenth century parliamentary speaker accused the assembly under Edward II of chattering and chirping in a way that calls to mind *The Owl and the Nightingale* (73, 76). Reed acknowledges that his poetic and institutional materials are contemporary with one another, with some of the institutional develop-ments occurring later (42). And if we recall our starting place—the debate in Homer's muses—it will remind us that dispute poetry has a long head start. Reed himself often directs attention to the long history of Western and Eastern precedents.

28. Walter Pater, "Conclusion," in *The Renaissance: Studies in Art and Poetry*, ed. Adam Phillips (Oxford: Oxford University Press, 1998), originally published in 1868; quoted and discussed by Harold Bloom in *The Anatomy of Influence: Literature as a Way of Life* (New Haven, CT: Yale University Press, 2011), 22.

29. The next three paragraphs provide a summary of arguments I make more fully in *On Beauty and Being Just* (Princeton, NJ: Princeton University Press, 1999), 3–5, 86, 93–116.

30. I am mainly speaking here about the aftermath of reading, but this lateralness is recognizable within the act of reading itself, as when one lets a character's worries take up the mental space usually reserved for one's own worries (here the work of beauty coincides with the work of empathy), or when one lends Proust one's mind for several weeks so he can create whatever pictures there he wishes, or when as a literary critic one makes oneself subordinate to the artist—John Keats—about whom one is writing.

31. Bernadette A. Meyler, "Daniel Defoe and the Written Constitution," *Cornell Law Review* 94 (2008): 73.

32. J. R. Maddicott, *The Origins of the English Parliament, 924–1327* (Oxford: Oxford University Press, 2010), vii, 3–7, 10, 16, 25, 26, 29, 31.

33. Sarah Foot, *Æthelstan: The First King of England* (New Haven, CT: Yale University Press, 2011), 95–96, 358, and see the chapter, "Æthelstan Patron of Poets," 101ff., esp. 106–108. Scholarly essays collected in Colin Chase's *The Dating of Beowulf* (Toronto: University of Toronto Press, 1981) present the rival arguments for the eighth, ninth, and tenth centuries. The case for Æthelstan is given by R. I. Page (113–22), E. G. Stanley (200–1), and Colin Chase citing Robert L. Reynolds, Norman Blake, and Nicolas Jacobs (7).

34. Foot, *Æthelstan*, 12.

35. This is why the State in Orwell's *1984* is not only intent on destroying facts, but gives equal priority to destroying fiction. Fiction nourishes the ongoing exercise of counterfactual thinking without which there cannot be thinking. I have argued this more fully in "A Defense of Poesy (The Treatise of Julia)," in *On Nineteen Eighty-Four: Orwell and Our Future*, ed. Abbott Gleason, Jack Goldsmith, and Martha C. Nussbaum (Princeton, NJ: Princeton University Press, 2005), 13–28.

THE ETHICS OF READING

1. J. Hillis Miller, *The Ethics of Reading* (New York: Columbia University Press, 1989).

2. I have discussed the matter in more detail in "Interpretation und Gespräch. Reflexionen zu Gadamers *Wahrheit und Methode*," in *Poetica* 43 (2011): 177–203.

3. E. D. Hirsch, *Validity in Interpretation* (New Haven, CT: Yale University Press, 1965). I criticize some of Hirsch's formulations in the essay cited in note 3.

4. Karl Kraus, "Die Sprache," in *Magie der Sprache* (Frankfurt: Suhrkamp, 1982): 344. "Einer geistigen Disziplin, die gegenüber dem einzigen, was ungestraft verletzt werden kann, der Sprache, das höchste Maß einer Verantwortung festsetzt und wie keine andere geeignet ist, den Respekt vor jeglichem andern Lebensgut zu lehren."

JONATHAN CULLER

1. Wayne Booth, "Epilogue: The Ethics of Reading," in *The Company We Keep: An Ethics of Fiction* (Berkeley: University of California Press, 1988): 489.

2. Marcel Proust, *Remembrance of Things Past*, vol. 1, trans. C.K. Scott Moncrieff (New York: Random House, 1981): 133–34.

3. Geoffrey G. Harpham, *Getting It Right: Language, Literature, and Ethics* (Chicago: University of Chicago Press, 1992): 142–3.

4. Jean-François Lyotard, *Differend: Phrases in Dispute*, trans. Georges Van Den Abbeele (Minneapolis: University of Minnesota Press, 1983).

5. Wayne Booth, *Literary Understanding: The Power and Limits of Pluralism* (Chicago: University of Chicago Press, 1979): 243.

6. G.K. Chesterton, *The Collected Works of G. K. Chesterton XV* (San Francisco: Ignatius Press, 1989): 213.

DISCUSSION SESSION I: THE ETHICS OF READING

1. *See* Suzanne Keen, "A Theory of Narrative Empathy," *Narrative* 14.3 (2006): 207–236; Suzanne Keen, *Empathy and the Novel* (Oxford: Oxford University Press, 2007).

2. George Makdisi, *The Rise of Colleges: Institutions of Learning in Islam and the West* (Edinburgh: Edinburgh University Press, 1981).

THE RAW AND THE HALF-COOKED

1. "A woman raises her arms for products as people loot from a destroyed shop after Tuesday's Earthquake in Port-au-Prince," January 16, 2010 (Reuters/Carlos Barria), www.boston.com/bigpicture/2010/01/haiti_six_ days_later.html.

2. "A mob of Haitians reach out as goods are thrown from a nearby shop in the downtown business district on January 17, 2010 in Port-au-Prince, Haiti" (Chris Hondros/Getty Images), www.boston.com/bigpicture/2010/01 /haiti_six_days_later.html.

3. "Looters throw a box with goods taken from a destroyed store in Port-au-Prince," January 18, 2010 (Reuters/Carlos Barria).

4. Over the last decade, the movement Personhood USA has tried to amend various state constitutions so that full personhood would be extended "to every human being at any stage of development." In 2011, Congressman Paul Ryan

[R-Wisconsin] sponsored a bill to amend the U.S. Constitution to include a clause that would read, "[T]he life of each human being begins with fertilization, cloning, or its functional equivalent, irrespective of sex, health, function or disability, defect, stage of biological development, or condition of dependency, at which time every human being shall have all the legal and constitutional attributes and privileges of personhood." Sanctity of Human Life Act, H.R. 212 (112th Congress, 2011–2012) and H.R. 23 (113th Congress 2013).

5. The platform stated, "We support a human life amendment to the Constitution and endorse legislation to make clear that the Fourteenth Amendment's protections apply to unborn children." Republican Platform 2012, 14; www.gop.com/2012-republican-platform_we.

6. *Citizens United v. Federal Election Commission*, 558 U.S. 310 (2010), held that corporations' expenditure of company funds for electioneering was a form of free speech and thus protected under the First Amendment. See also *Buckley v. Valeo*, 424 U.S. 1 (1976), holding that individuals' expenditures of money constitutes protected political speech.

7. Dalina Castellanos, "Geraldo Rivera: Hoodie Responsible for Trayvon Martin's Death," *Los Angeles Times*, March 23, 2012.

8. Elizabeth Flock, "Geraldo Rivera Hoodie Comments Spark Prominent People to Wear Hoodies," *Washington Post*, March 27, 2012.

9. "To do justice, and to love mercy, and to walk humbly with your God. . . ." (Micah 6:8); Lisa Miller, "Trayvon Martin: Doing Justice, Having Faith in Social Media," *Washington Post*, March 29, 2012. See also Rosalind Helderman, "Rep. Bobby Rush Chided for Wearing Hoodie on House Floor for Trayvon Martin," *Washington Post*, March 28, 2012.

10. "During the session of the House, a Member, Delegate, or Resident Commissioner may not wear a hat or remain by the Clerk's desk during the call of the roll or the counting of ballots. . . . The Sergeant-at-Arms is charged with the strict enforcement of this clause."

11. Peter Grier, "Why Couldn't Rep. Bobby Rush Wear Hoodie on House Floor?" *Christian Science Monitor*, March 28, 2012.

12. M. Norton and S. Sommers, "Whites See Racism as a Zero-Sum Game That They Are Now Losing," *Perspectives on Psychological Science* 6 (2011): 215–218.

13. Saidiya Hartman, "Venus in Two Acts," *Small Axe* 26 (2008): 3.

CONQUERING THE OBSTACLES TO KINGDOM AND FATE: THE ETHICS OF READING AND THE UNIVERSITY ADMINISTRATOR

1. *See* description of *elenchus* at http://plato.stanford.edu/entries/plato -ethics-shorter/.

2. *See* Matthew 22:15–22; Mark 12:13–17; Luke 20:19–26.

WILLIAM GERMANO

1. Gerald Graff, *Clueless in Academe: How Schooling Obscures the Life of the Mind* (New Haven, CT: Yale University Press, 2003), 10.

DISCUSSION SESSION 2: THE ETHICS OF READING AND THE PROFESSIONS

1. Kenneth Burke, "The Rhetoric of Hitler's 'Battle,'" in *The Philosophy of Literary Form: Studies in Symbolic Action*, 3rd ed. (Berkeley: University of California Press, 1973), 191–220.

2. United States Department of Justice, Memorandum for John Rizzo, "Interrogation of al Qaeda Operative," August 1, 2002, 14; http://documents .nytimes.com/justice-department-memos-on-interrogation-techniques.

THE CALL OF ANOTHER'S WORDS

1. Frank Bird Linderman, *American: The Life Story of a Great Indian, Plenty-Coups, Chief of the Crows* (New York: John Day, 1930).

2. Jonathan Lear, *Radical Hope: Ethics in the Face of Cultural Devastation* (Cambridge, MA: Harvard University Press, 2006).

RESPONSES AND DISCUSSION

1. Serguei Alex Oushakine, "The Terrifying Mimicry of Samizdat," *Public Culture* 13, no. 2 (2001): 191–214.

2. Jaroslav Hašek, *The Good Soldier Švejk*, trans. Cecil Parrott (London: Penguin, 1974).

3. Ibid., 18.

4. Ibid., 19, phrase translated in original (1911).

5. *See, e.g.* Megan R. Martin, "The Growth of Czech Feminism through Resistance Activities from 1968 to 1993," *Newsletter of the Institute of Slavic, East European, and Eurasian Studies*, 26, no 1 (Spring 2009): 7–13.

6. István Örkény, *Egyperces novella* (Hungary 1967); translated here by Kim Lane Scheppele.

DIDIER FASSIN

1. Joseph Conrad, *Heart of Darkness* (New York: Penguin, 1902/1994), 72.

DISCUSSION SESSION 3: THE HUMANITIES AND HUMAN RIGHTS

1. Kevin O'Flynn, "Toys Cannot Hold Protest Because They Are Not Citizens of Russia, Officials Rule," *The Guardian*, February 15, 2012.

2. Charles Baudelaire, "A Philosophy of Toys," in *The Painter of Modern Life and Other Essays*, ed. and trans. Jonathan Mayne (London: Phaidon, 1964), 198–99; originally published as "Morale du joujou," *Monde Littéraire*, April 17, 1853.

3. Elaine Scarry, *The Body in Pain: The Making and Unmaking of the World* (New York: Oxford University Press, 1985).

CONCLUDING DISCUSSION

1. Mark Payne, *The Animal Part: Human and Other Animals in the Poetic Imagination* (Chicago: University of Chicago Press, 2010).

2. Conversation between Daniel Callahan (co-founder of Hastings Center) and Elaine Scarry, Hasting Center, Garrison, New York, December 6, 1980. See also Bernard Rosen and Arthur Caplan, *Ethics in the Undergraduate Curriculum* (New York: Hastings Center, 1980); Daniel Callahan and Sissela Bok, *Ethics Teaching in Higher Education* (New York: Hasting Center, 1980); Charles Radey, "Telling Stories: Creative Literature and Ethics," *Hastings Center Report* 20, no. 6 (November–December 1990), 25.

3. Geoffrey Galt Harpham, *The Humanities and the Dream of America* (Chicago: University of Chicago Press, 2011).

4. Christian Thorne, *The Dialectic of Counter-Enlightenment* (Cambridge, MA, Harvard University Press, 2009).

KWAME ANTHONY APPIAH is Laurance S. Rockefeller University Professor in Philosophy and the University Center for Human Values at Princeton University. He has published widely in philosophy and in African and African American literary and cultural studies. His recent books include *Thinking It Through: An Introduction to Contemporary Philosophy* (2004), *The Ethics of Identity* (2005), *Cosmopolitanism: Ethics in a World of Strangers* (2006), *Experiments in Ethics* (2008), and *The Honor Code: How Moral Revolutions Happen* (2010).

DEREK ATTRIDGE is Professor of English at The University of York. He is the author of, among other titles, *Moving Words: Forms of English Poetry* (2013), *Reading and Responsibility: Deconstruction's Traces* (2010), and *J.M. Coetzee and The Ethics of Reading* (2004).

PETER BROOKS is Andrew W. Mellon Foundation Scholar at Princeton University, and Sterling Professor Emeritus of Comparative Literature at Yale University. His essays and reviews have appeared in *The New York Times, The New Republic, Times Literary Supplement, The Nation, New York Review of Books, Critical Inquiry, New Literary History, Yale Journal of Law and Humanities*, and elsewhere. He is the author of numerous books, including *Enigmas of Identity* (2011), *Henry James Goes to Paris* (2007), *Realist Vision* (2005), *Troubling Confessions* (2000), *Psychoanalysis and Storytelling* (1994), *Body Work* (1993), and *Reading for the Plot* (1984).

JUDITH BUTLER is Wun Tsun Tam Mellon Visiting Professor of the Humanities at Columbia University and Maxine Elliot Professor in the Departments of Rhetoric and Comparative Literature and the Co-director of the Program of Critical Theory at the University of California, Berkeley. She is the author of, among other titles, *Gender Trouble: Feminism and the Subversion of Identity* (1990), *The Psychic Life of Power: Theories of Subjection* (1997), *Precarious Life: Powers of Violence and Mourning* (2004); *Undoing Gender* (2004), *Giving an Account of Oneself* (2005), *Frames of War: When Is Life Grievable?* (2009), and *Parting Ways* (2012).

Jonathan Culler is Class of 1916 Professor of English at Cornell University. He is the author of, among other books, *Structuralist Poetics: Structuralism, Linguistics, and the Study of Literature* (1975), *On Deconstruction* (1982 and 2007), and *The Pursuit of Signs: Semiotics, Literature, Deconstruction* (2001).

Didier Fassin is James D. Wolfensohn Professor of Social Science at the Institute for Advanced Study in Princeton and Director of Studies at the Ecole des Hautes Etudes en Sciences Sociales in Paris. Recent publications include: *When Bodies Remember: Experiences and Politics of AIDS in South Africa* (2007), *The Empire of Trauma: An Inquiry into the Condition of Victimhood* (2009), *Humanitarian Reason: A Moral History of the Present* (2011), and *Enforcing Order: An Ethnography of Urban Policing* (2013).

William Germano is Professor and Dean of the Faculty of the Humanities and Social Sciences at Cooper Union. Prior to joining Cooper Union, he directed programs in scholarly publishing as editor-in-chief at Columbia University Press and as vice-president and publishing director at Routledge. Publications include *Getting it Published: A Guide for Scholars and Anyone Else Serious about Serious Books* (2008), *From Dissertation to Book* (2013) and *The Tales of Hoffman* (2013).

Ralph Hexter is Distinguished Professor of Classics and Comparative Literature and Provost and Executive Vice Chancellor at the University of California, Davis. He came to Davis from Hampshire College in Amherst, Massachusetts, where he was President; prior to that, he served as Dean of Arts & Humanities at the University of California, Berkeley. Publications include *The Oxford Handbook of Medieval Latin Literature* (2012, edited with David Townsend) and *A Guide to the Odyssey: A Commentary on the English Translation of Robert Fitzgerald* (1993).

Paul W. Kahn is Robert W. Winner Professor of Law and the Humanities, and Director of the Orville H. Schell, Jr. Center for International Human Rights at Yale Law School. He is the author of, among other books, *Political Theology: Four New Chapters on the Concept of Sovereignty* (2011); *Sacred Violence: Torture, Terror, and Sovereignty* (2008); *The Cultural Study of Law: Reconstructing Legal Scholarship* (1999); and *Marbury v. Madison and the Construction of America* (1997).

Charles Larmore is W. Duncan MacMillan Family Professor in the Humanities at Brown University. He is the author of, among other books, *The Morals of Modernity* (1996); *Les Pratiques du moi* (2004, awarded the "Grand Prix de Philosophie" by the Académie Française); *Débat sur l'éthique* (2004, co-authored with Alain Renaut); *The Autonomy of Morality* (2008); and *Dernières nouvelles du moi* (2009, co-authored with Vincent Descombes). His most recent book, *Vernunft und Subjektivität* (2012), is on the nature of reason.

JONATHAN LEAR is John U. Nef Distinguished Service Professor in the Committee on Social Thought and the Department of Philosophy at the University of Chicago. He works primarily on philosophical conceptions of the human psyche from Socrates to the present. He also serves on the faculties of the Chicago Institute for Psychoanalysis and the Western New England Institute for Psychoanalysis. His numerous books include: *Open Minded: Working out the Logic of the Soul* (1999), *Therapeutic Action: An Earnest Plea for Irony* (2003), *Radical Hope: Ethics in the Face of Cultural Devastation* (2008), and *A Case for Irony* (2011).

MICHAEL ROTH is President of Wesleyan University. He has published and taught widely in history and the humanities. Among his articles and books are *Psycho-Analysis as History: Negation and Freedom in Freud* (1987, 1995); *The Ironist's Cage: Trauma, Memory and the Construction of History* (1995), and *Memory, Trauma, and History: Essays on Living with the Past* (2011). He is at work on a new book, *Why Liberal Education Matters*.

ELAINE SCARRY is Walter M. Cabot Professor of Aesthetics and General Theory of Value at Harvard University. She is the author of numerous books, most notably *Thinking in an Emergency* (2011); *On Beauty and Being Just* (1999); *Literature and the Body* (1988); and *The Body in Pain: The Making and Unmaking of the World* (1985).

KIM LANE SCHEPPELE is Director of the Program in Law and Public Affairs at Princeton University and Laurance S. Rockefeller Professor of Sociology and International Affairs in the Woodrow Wilson School and the University Center for Human Values. Her many publications on both post-1989 constitutional transitions and on post-9/11 constitutional challenges have appeared in law reviews, social science journals and in many languages (including Russian, Hungarian and French). Her forthcoming book is *The International State of Emergency: Constitutional Exceptions and the Globalization of Security Law after 9/11* (2014).

RICHARD SENNETT is University Professor of Sociology at New York University and Professor of Sociology at the London School of Economics. His work explores how individuals and groups make sense of the material facts within which they live and work. Among his many works are *The Uses of Disorder* (1970), *The Corrosion of Character* (1998), *The Craftsman* (2008) and *Together: The Rituals, Pleasures and Politics of Cooperation* (2012).

PATRICIA WILLIAMS is James L. Dohr Professor of Law at Columbia Law School. She has published widely in the areas of race, gender, and law, and on other issues of legal theory and justice. She is a regular columnist with *The Nation.* Her books include *The Alchemy of Race and Rights* (1991). *The Rooster's Egg* (1995) and *Seeing a ColorBlind Future: The Paradox of Race* (1997).

HILARY JEWETT (coeditor) holds a Ph.D. in Comparative Literature from Yale University and a J.D. from the Benjamin N. Cardozo School of Law. She has taught literary theory at Yale and Brown and practiced law in New York City. She helped to coordinate the symposium on "The Humanities in the Public Sphere" at Princeton University, on which this book is based.